# nadiya bakes

michael joseph
*an imprint* of
penguin books

For Abdal

*If you didn't eat cake, who would
I bake cake for?*

*This cake was always going
to be for you.*

# NADIYA BAKES

nadiya hussain

photography by **chris terry**

# contents

# introduction

**As first loves go, I have many. We all have many.**

For fifteen-year-old me, it was the Backstreet Boys, who I was going to meet one day (so I told myself) and I would marry Kevin, though not before all five of them battled to win my love! Even now, at thirty-five, they still send my heart a flutter because out of all the bands that fifteen-year-old girl could have loved, they were the first.

But back here in real life, away from the land of make-believe and distant teenage dreams, I have had the joy of many weird and wonderful first loves. Becoming a proper older sister, when my baby brother was born, my first taste of maternal, yet not technically maternal, love. That was a first love of many to come. My first real pet, Hira the cat, she loved me like tuna and I loved her like I love crisps. Becoming an aunt for the very first time, that rush of connection: we share the same DNA and I didn't even have a hand in making him. That was a first love.

My first second-hand bike I shared with my sisters; her name was Bluebird and she was blue, rusty, with white tyres and cost my dad 30p from a Sunday market. I loved that bike, but that unpadded seat did not love me! My first pair of roller skates, yes they were hand-me-downs and I grew out of them pretty sharpish, but they rolled me to places beyond the parameters set by parental guidance, not far but far enough, so my blades I loved.

Finding love, actual real love, nothing like anyone else's and all our own. Real, first, true, actual love. And children: real people, growing inside me, waiting to be met. You would think that first love of seeing one's child would change, fade or lessen with each subsequent child, but no. It's still there, first love, fresh love, new love, every single time, with every single child.

## And then of course there is cake. Yes, cake.

You may ask, how can cake sit here in this list? This list of monumental events and material memories, where does cake fit here? Like everything on my list of first loves, baking came into my life at a particular point, but unlike my memories of boy bands, roller-blades and pets, which sit somewhere in 'things that once were', baking is right here with me still. With my husband, with my children, with my family. Baking has become such a massive part of who I am that there is no denying it. I live it, I breathe it, I whisk, stir, measure and bake it! For goodness' sake, I dream about it! I really do.

Baking is my first love.

I didn't quite realize it when as a teenager I baked a cake for my sister's pre-wedding party. A simple sponge, sandwiched together with sticky jam and groaning under the sheer weight of thick white fondant and a hideous fondant groom all dressed in his fondant finery. I didn't see it when I did a GCSE in Food Studies a few years later and designed an entire Pokémon Cake, with marbled red-and-white sponge, sand-wiched with jam and covered in a coloured fondant, shaped and cut carefully to create an actual 'Poké Ball'. The teacher said, 'You're really good at baking. Ever considered going to catering college?' I'm also

good at tying my shoelaces, so who cares?! I thought. I just wanted an A in Food Studies and that I got. But still nothing – the connection wasn't there. Whatever it is I have now, whatever I feel now, it didn't ignite, it didn't even spark.

We had an oven at home, but it was full of pans; it wasn't used for baking, just for storing greasy deep-frying pans and I never really saw it any other way. It was a cupboard NOT an oven. Life happened around all of that – I got married and we got our own house and even our own oven. Still nothing, not an urge, not a spark, not a thought to bake. Until...

'Can you bake, because I love cake?' I supposed I *could* bake, maybe just a little, for him. I gave it a try. It started with a wonky sponge, and he ate the whole thing. So I saved for an oven thermometer to make sure the oven temperature was regulated. The next cake was less wonky. Still delicious and he ate it again! Then some strawberry and cream muffins. A whole dozen. A little chewy, not very cake-like, tasty though, and he ate them all. By then the babies joined in too. I saved a few strawberries out of sight in the back of the fridge and tried again. Mixed the mixture a little less. There was a definite improvement. They were eaten even faster than the ones that came before.

And before I knew it I was baking bread, enriching doughs, making pastry, laminating, making starters – and killing starters! I was baking every day, all because I had someone to eat it. Baking became a part of life, like cooking, like laundry, like hoovering, like breathing. It was just natural, it was normal. And it was loved.

So nothing gives me greater pleasure than to finally be able to share this beautiful book with you. I could have begun writing this book and never really stopped, but the powers that be said I had to! So I did. But not till I had put together some of my favourite recipes, traditional, twisted and everything in between. This book is a compilation of all the yummy ideas that fly around in my head and all the things my husband eats over and over again.

Let me take you through the chapters. Cakes, Mini Cakes & Traybakes: if you're in this chapter I would highly recommend the money can't buy you happiness brownies. If you're in the No-bake Bakes chapter, well you guessed right: no baking but still 'baking' with the banana ice cream cheesecake with blueberry compote. Tarts & Pies: this is filled with all sorts of delights from a sweet carrot tart to a rainbow veg pakora picnic pie. Desserts: you'll need a spoon in this chapter, if you're eating the roasted fruit cobbler or the croissant and ice cream pudding. Every baker needs a good Celebration Bake and there are plenty to pick from. It could be a sit-in-the-middle-of-the-table cranberry and chilli brioche wreath or a celebratory praline king cake. We can't have a baking book without a Breads chapter, full of Cornish splits and pulled chicken doughnuts. Biscuits, we've got to have biscuits, be they coffee meringue bark or rhubarb and custard butter kisses! If you fancy a Savoury Bake there are baked chilli churros and a cauliflower cheese lasagne. There is something in this book for all of us for every occasion – not that we need an occasion to turn on the oven!

Many people may read this and not get it. But for those of you who love baking as much as I do, you will get it instantly and that's why you now have this book in your home. Baking doesn't have to be your first love, or indeed anywhere in a long list of loves like mine, but perhaps it's waiting to become one of yours, and maybe you'll find just the recipe in here to ignite the love or at the very least fuel it.

**Bake, eat, love, repeat!**

# chapter one

# CAKES,
# MINI CAKES &
# TRAYBAKES

# turmeric and ginger diamonds

Makes approx. 24 diamonds
Prep 20 minutes   Cook 30 minutes
Will keep for 5 days in a tin

This is my take on a traditional Lebanese treat. The turmeric smells savoury, but in fact it brings a sweetness to the recipe, and I have also added ginger to really complement the turmeric, so your senses will be very busy. These look beautiful and are so simple to make, topped with pine nuts and sesame seeds for some crunch. Perfect if you want something a little bit different.

### for the cake

80g tahini

375g plain flour, sifted

300g caster sugar

2 teaspoons ground ginger

2 teaspoons turmeric

½ teaspoon baking powder

120ml good olive oil

350ml boiling water

2 large chunks of stem ginger, washed and very finely chopped, reserving 4 tablespoons of syrup from the jar

### for the top

1 tablespoon sesame seeds

1 tablespoon pine nuts

Start by preheating the oven to 180°C/fan 160°C/gas 4. Have a 20 x 30cm brownie tin ready, lined with baking paper.

Add the tahini straight into the base of the brownie tin and, using a pastry brush, brush the sides and edges until they are completely covered.

Add the flour, sugar, ginger, turmeric and baking powder to a bowl and whisk till combined.

Make a well in the centre and add the olive oil, then the boiling water, then the stem ginger and mix until you have a beautifully fragrant yellow batter, thick enough to pour.

Now pour the mixture into the tahini-lined tray – it should all run into a smooth, even layer. Sprinkle the sesame and pine nuts all over the top.

Bake for 30 minutes until firm to the touch. Take it out of the oven and leave for 10 minutes before using a small serrated knife to cut diagonal lines in opposite directions, still in the tin, to form diamonds.

Brush all over with about 4 tablespoons of the syrup from the stem ginger.

Leave to cool completely in the tin before serving.

# blueberry and lavender scone pizza

**Makes** 12 wedges   **Prep** 25 minutes
**Cook** 15 minutes   **Best eaten** straight away

**For the scone**

350g self-raising flour, sifted, plus a little extra for dusting

a pinch of salt

1 teaspoon baking powder

85g unsalted butter, softened

45g caster sugar

1 teaspoon dried lavender, crushed

1 lemon, zest only

175ml whole milk, room temperature

**For the topping**

2 x 227g clotted cream

1 teaspoon vanilla bean paste

100g blueberry jam

180g fresh blueberries

zest of half a lemon

These scone wedges are made in one big circle, just like a pizza. The dough is lightly scented with lavender and topped with rippled cream and jam and lots of fresh blueberries. I am forever getting involved in the what-goes-first debate (cream or jam?), though to be honest as long as neither is left off, I'm a happy girl. I once vowed never again to bake with lavender after an epic flavour disaster, but I have since learnt that a little goes a long way. So, don't be tempted to divert from the quantities here, or you WILL regret it!

Preheat the oven to 200°C/fan 180°C/gas 6 and line a large baking tray with baking paper.

Pop the flour into a large bowl, along with the salt and baking powder, and mix through.

Add the butter and rub it into the flour using your fingertips until there are no large traces left. Add the sugar, dried lavender and lemon zest and mix.

Make a well in the centre and add the milk. Using a palette knife, mix until it starts to form a dough. Gently bring the dough together with your hands. Tip it out onto a lightly floured surface and form the dough into a mound, but resist the temptation to knead or the scone will become chewy rather than soft and crumbly.

Put the mound into the centre of the prepared tray – this just saves a messy transfer once the dough is rolled out. Using a rolling pin or the back of your hand, press the dough out to a large circle about 2cm thick. If you want, trim the edges, though I prefer not to as I like the edges rough.

Now, using a sharp knife, cut the circle like a pizza into 12 slices, cutting all the way down and all the way through. Pop into the oven and bake for 15 minutes. The scone should be golden around the edges, a little less so towards the centre, and firm to the touch.

Leave to cool completely on the tray. As soon as it is cool enough, pop it onto your chosen serving dish.

Mix the clotted cream and vanilla bean paste together. Add the jam and ripple it right the way through.

Spread the mixture all over the scone, leaving a 1cm gap around the edge, like a pizza crust, so you'll have somewhere cream-free to hold. Top with blueberries, scatter with lemon zest, and you are ready to serve!

cakes, mini cakes & traybakes

# tahini cake
## with banana curd

**Serves** 8–10  **Prep** 40 minutes
**Cook** 1 hour

**For the cake**

butter for greasing

200g tahini

200g caster sugar

4 medium eggs

1 medium banana, squashed to a paste, about 100g

200g self-raising flour, sifted

1 teaspoon baking powder

1 teaspoon vanilla extract

**For the curd**

4 medium eggs

60g unsalted butter, softened

2 tablespoons lemon juice

300g caster sugar

4 medium bananas, ripe, about 400g

1 tablespoon cornflour

½ teaspoon nutmeg

**For the crunch**

2 x 30g packs of sesame snaps, crushed

This cake is made with tahini, so it is deliciously light and – like most of us – subtly nutty! The banana curd is scented lightly with nutmeg, so it's sweet with a bit of depth – again like most of us. Sesame brittle adds a crunch in places. I think we have established that we are all a little bit tahini cake with banana curd!

Start by lining a 900g loaf tin with some baking paper and lightly greasing it. Preheat the oven to 160°C/fan 140°C/gas 3.

Put the tahini, sugar, eggs, banana, flour, baking powder and vanilla into a large mixing bowl and whizz together with an electric hand whisk for two minutes until the mixture is smooth and glossy. Pour into the prepared loaf tin and level off the top.

Bake in the oven on the middle shelf for 1 hour until it has domed, is a light brown, and a skewer inserted comes out clean.

While it bakes, make the curd by putting the eggs, butter, lemon juice, sugar, bananas, cornflour and nutmeg into a food processor and blitzing to a smooth paste.

Transfer the mix into a non-stick pan and place over a medium heat, stirring all the time, until the mixture has thickened. Take it off the heat, transfer to a bowl and leave to cool completely, then cover with cling-film and chill in the fridge.

As soon as the cake is ready, take it out and leave it to cool on a wire rack.

Cut the cooled cake twice horizontally, so you have three even layers. Set the top two layers aside and cover the bottom layer with two heaped tablespoons of curd, spread evenly. Sprinkle over a third of the crushed sesame snaps. Add the next cake layer and spread it with curd. Add another third of the crushed sesame snaps. Put the top layer of the cake back on and spread it with curd (about 5 tablespoons), then sprinkle over the rest of the crushed sesame snaps.

Any leftover curd will sit pretty in a jar for 2 weeks. Perfect for pancakes!

# matcha and kiwi hurricane roll

butter to grease

**For the plain sponge**

4 medium eggs

100g caster sugar

100g self-raising flour, sifted

**For the matcha sponge**

4 medium eggs

100g caster sugar

90g plain flour, sifted

2 tablespoons matcha powder

**For the filling**

4 kiwi fruit, peeled and roughly chopped

55g icing sugar

150g thick double cream

**Serves** 8–10   **Prep** 40 minutes
**Cook** 15–18 minutes   **Best eaten** on day it's made

This is a Swiss roll taken to the next level by adding a bright green ripple of matcha-flavoured sponge for an amazing hurricane effect. It's a thing of beauty! The distinctive matcha flavour in the sponge is paired with a fruity kiwi cream in the centre, and topped with a kiwi coulis. Too beautiful to eat? I think not.

Start by preheating the oven to 180°C/fan 160°C/gas 4, and grease and line a 30 x 40cm baking tray with some baking paper.

Now, begin making the plain sponge. In a large mixing bowl whisk the eggs and sugar together until the mixture is really light and fluffy and the whisk leaves a trail when lifted – this is how you can tell it is thick enough. It should take 5 minutes using an electric hand whisk.

Next, add the flour and, using a spatula, gently fold the mixture together until there are no trails of flour left and you have a smooth, airy batter.

Pour the mixture into the prepared tin and tilt it around to get the mixture into all the corners. Set it aside while you make the matcha mix.

Follow the same initial process as before, whisking the eggs and sugar together until the mixture is thick and the whisk leaves a trail. Add the flour and matcha and fold gently together until you have a smooth, deep-green cake batter.

Pop the mixture into a piping bag – this will just make it easier to layer the green batter on top of the plain one in the tray without too much accidental mixing. Snip off the end and pipe the mixture over the top (see overleaf for the pattern).

Position the tray with the longest edge closest to you. Now take a table knife, skewer or a small rounded spoon and, starting at one corner, stick it in until it

→

touches the base of the tin and run it through the batter all the way from end to end with one firm, continuous movement. When you get to the end, make a U-turn and go back, then another U-turn and back again, as if you are doing lengths of a pool, while gradually moving in a zigzag across the breadth of the whole tray.

Keep doing this until you have gone all the way across the tray.

Rotate the tray by 90 degrees so that now the shortest edge is closest to you and do the same in the other direction until you have gone all the way across.

Finally, give the tray two sharp taps on the worktop to help the mixture settle and make the top look more uniform.

Pop into the oven and bake for 15–18 minutes until the centre is springy to the touch.

Have ready a large sheet of baking paper spread with a generous amount of caster sugar.

As soon as you have taken the sponge out of the oven, tip it out onto the sugared paper.

The cake will be sandwiched between two sheets of baking paper; loosen the top sheet and then pop it back in place. Now, starting from the longer edge, roll up the whole thing, paper and all, and leave to cool completely.

Next, make the filling by adding the kiwi to a food processor along with the icing sugar and blitzing to a smooth paste.

Once the cake has cooled, unravel it, remove the topmost sheet of baking paper and spread half of the kiwi purée all over. Whisk the cream lightly, so it just holds its shape, then spread that over the kiwi in a thin layer. Now roll the whole thing back up again.

Reserve the rest of the kiwi purée for the top.

Take off the scrappy ends – they are for you, you're welcome! This just neatens up the roll so you can see the hurricane effect.

Pop onto a serving dish, drizzle over the rest of the kiwi purée in a line across the top and let it drip, slice and you are ready to eat.

→

# money can't buy you happiness brownies

**Makes** 18 squares
**Prep** 40 minutes, plus overnight chilling
**Cook** 55 minutes **Best kept** in the fridge for 3–4 days

**For the brownie base**

250g unsalted butter, softened, plus extra to grease

250g dark chocolate

4 medium eggs

280g soft dark brown sugar

1 teaspoon instant coffee mixed with 2 teaspoons hot water

120g plain flour, sifted

30g cocoa, sifted

½ teaspoon salt

1 teaspoon plain flour

150g dark choc chips

**For the nutty centre**

1 x 450g jar of dulce de leche

200g chopped mixed nuts or hazelnuts

½ teaspoon salt

**For the top**

300g full-fat soft cream cheese

100g caster sugar

2 medium eggs

1 teaspoon almond extract

zest of 1 orange

1 tablespoon plain flour

cocoa powder for dusting

I don't think I need to elaborate too much on these, do I? I am always in search of the best brownie, and I figure if you can't find it, make it. So here it is: a triple chocolate brownie, with a layer of toasted chopped nuts encased in dulce de leche, then topped with a zesty cheesecake mixture and baked again. I rest my case.

Put the butter and chocolate in a small pan and melt gently, stirring occasionally until the mixture is liquid. Set aside to cool.

Line the base and sides of a 20 x 30 x 5cm brownie tin with some baking paper so that it comes 1cm above the top of the tin, and lightly grease.

Preheat the oven to 180°C/fan 160°C/gas 4.

Add the eggs, sugar and cooled coffee to a large mixing bowl and whisk until the mixture is light, thick and fluffy. This should take 5 minutes with an electric hand whisk. (Adding the coffee really enhances the flavour of the cocoa and you won't even be able to taste the coffee itself.)

Pour in the cooled melted chocolate and whisk until the mixture no longer has any streaks in it.

Then add the sifted flour, cocoa and salt and mix until you have a glossy batter.

Mix the teaspoon of flour with the chocolate chips in a bowl before mixing them into the batter until they're well dispersed – this trick will stop them sinking to the bottom when you bake the brownies. Pour the mixture into the prepared tin and level off the top. Bake for 25 minutes.

While it is baking, toast the nuts in a large non-stick pan, stirring until they are a deep golden brown.

Put the dulce de leche in a bowl along with the toasted nuts and the salt, mix and set aside.

As soon as the brownies are baked, take them out of the oven and leave to cool completely in the tin. As soon as they have cooled, spread the sticky nut

mixture over the top and pop the whole thing in the freezer for 30 minutes.

Adjust the oven to 170°C/fan 150°C/gas 3½.

Make the cheesecake top by mixing the cream cheese, sugar, egg, almond extract, orange zest and flour together really well.

Spoon and spread into an even layer over the nut mixture and pop into the oven for 30 minutes.

As soon as the cheesecake is set in the centre, allow to cool totally and leave in the fridge overnight. The wait will be worth it!

Dust with the cocoa, take out of the tin and cut into squares. Eat, eat, eat!

# torta caprese

## with caramelized white chocolate sauce

5 medium eggs, separated

a pinch of salt

200g unsalted butter, softened, plus extra for greasing

180g caster sugar

200g ground almonds

200g dark chocolate, melted

25g cocoa powder

1 teaspoon baking powder

icing sugar for dusting

**For the caramelized white chocolate**

400g good-quality white chocolate, broken into pieces

a pinch of salt

icing sugar

frozen summer fruit (optional)

Serves 8   **Prep** 30 minutes   **Cook** 1 hour, plus 45 minutes cooling   **Best eaten** while still a little warm but keeps well for 3 days

This is such a lovely chocolate cake, rich but light from whipped egg whites and yet with plenty of texture from the ground almonds. It's simple and delicious and so yummy served with warm caramelized white chocolate, as the only way my husband eats chocolate cake is with more chocolate on top!

Preheat the oven to 170°C/fan 150°C/gas 3½ and line and lightly grease a round 23cm cake tin.

Begin with two medium-sized bowls – separate the egg yolks and egg whites.

Add a pinch of salt to the egg whites and set aside.

Now take the bowl with the egg yolks and add the butter, sugar, ground almonds, cooled melted dark chocolate, cocoa powder and baking powder.

Return to the egg whites. Using a hand-held whisk, whisk until you have stiff peaks.

Now pop the beaters into the other mixture and whisk until you have a smooth, evenly blended chocolatey mixture.

Add a third of the egg white mixture into the chocolatey mix and mix in well with a spoon to loosen it.

Now add the rest of the egg white and gently fold in until you don't see any streaks remaining.

Pour into the prepared cake tin, level off the top and bake for 50 minutes–1 hour.

Now's a good time to begin making the caramelized white chocolate sauce to go with the torta.

Put the chocolate chunks or chips with a pinch of salt into a large non-stick pan, big enough so the chocolate is in an even-ish layer. Pop the pan on a low heat and allow the chocolate to melt completely.

Stir, and if all the chocolate has melted, spread out to an even, melted layer and turn up the heat just a fraction. Stir again and keep doing the same until all the chocolate is caramelized and an even golden colour.

If the chocolate stiffens to a solid, chalky lump, remove from the heat and leave to cool undisturbed for a couple of minutes until it starts to melt again then return to the heat and continue with spreading out and stirring. This whole process can take 20–25 minutes, and just as a warning, chocolate can get really hot so be very careful. It is quite a lumpy mixture so pop it into a jug or bowl, add 150ml hot water and whizz it with a stick blender and that should give you a smooth, caramelized white chocolate sauce.

Once the torta is baked it should be just firm in the centre. Turn the oven off, open the door and leave the torta in there for 30 minutes. Take out and leave to cool in the tin for another 15 minutes, then dust generously with icing sugar. By generously, I mean totally covered! Slice and serve with the warm caramelized white chocolate and frozen summer fruit if you like.

If the sauce has cooled and become solid you just need to reheat very gently in a pan or in a heatproof bowl over a pan of simmering water.

# strawberry and clotted cream shortcake cupcakes

Makes 12    Prep 30 minutes, plus chilling
Cook 15 minutes    Best kept in the fridge for up to 2 days

**For the strawberry ice-cream frosting**

175g slightly salted butter, softened

350g icing sugar

100g strawberry ice cream, softened

**For the cake**

12 round vanilla sandwich cookies

12 small to medium strawberries

110g clotted cream

110g caster sugar

2 medium eggs

1 teaspoon vanilla bean paste

110g self-raising flour, sifted

9g tube of freeze-dried strawberries to decorate

These are an American–British hybrid. I just can't settle on one flavour combo once I've thought of a way to combine several. Strawberries and cream is a classic, but I love clotted cream, so I couldn't resist using it to make the cake batter here: no butter, just cream! I also love strawberry short-cake, so under each cake is a biscuit base, then a hidden strawberry inside, and I've topped it all off with strawberry ice-cream frosting! Why have just one thing when you can have it all?

Begin by making the icing, as this needs chilling. Whisk the butter with an electric hand whisk until pale and creamy. Sift in the icing sugar. Stir with a spoon to roughly combine and then beat with the electric whisk until light and fluffy. Add the ice cream and whisk until just combined. Chill in the fridge for at least 1 hour.

Whisk the chilled icing until fluffy then transfer to a piping bag fitted with a 1cm star nozzle and put it back in the fridge while you get on with the baking.

Preheat the oven to 180°C/fan 160°C/gas 4 and line a 12-hole large muffin tray with some cupcake cases of your choice. To the base of each one, add a cookie, then top that with a whole strawberry, pointy bit facing up.

Now make the cake batter by adding the clotted cream and sugar to a mixing bowl and beating them together until light and fluffy.

Add the eggs one at a time, mixing well after each one.

Add the vanilla bean paste and flour and mix until you have a smooth batter.

Divide the mixture up between the 12 cases, making sure that each delicious strawberry is fully encased, until you have no batter left.

Tap the tray on the work surface to level off the batter and bake for 15 minutes, until they are fluffy and golden.

Take out and leave in the tin for 10 minutes before transferring them to a cooling rack.

Pipe the frosting onto the tops of the cupcakes and then sprinkle with the freeze-dried strawberries.

# upside-down key lime cupcakes

1 large lime, cut into 12 thin slices, then cut each slice in half

12 oat biscuits or ginger snaps (something that will fit the top part of the cupcake liner snugly)

whippy cream to serve (optional)

**For the cake**

55g unsalted butter, very soft

55g caster sugar

1 medium egg

½ teaspoon vanilla extract

55g self-raising flour, sieved

**For the lime custard layer**

200g condensed milk

1 medium egg

2 limes, zest and juice

150ml thick double cream

---

Makes 12    Prep 30 minute, plus cooling and chilling    Cook 25 minutes
Will keep in the fridge for up to 3 days

---

These are inspired by key lime pie, but in cake form and a little bit upside down. Each one is layered up in a cupcake case: lime, cake, zesty custard and biscuit, then baked and flipped over. All the same flavours as the famous pie, but literally turned on its head.

Start by preheating the oven to 180°C/fan 160°C/gas 4. Have a 12-hole deep muffin tray at the ready lined with some cupcake cases.

Place 2 lime half slices flat in the base of each cupcake case.

Now make the cake batter by adding the butter, sugar, egg, vanilla and flour to a bowl and whisking until you have a light and shiny batter.

Using a teaspoon, spoon a small amount into each cupcake case until you have run out of mixture, making sure to keep them fairly equal. The batter is very thick, so you will need to use the back of the spoon to spread it to the edges of the cases.

Give the tray a few hard slams on the work surface to level the batter, then pop into the oven for 10 minutes.

When they are done, take them out and leave to cool in the tin. Reduce the oven temperature to 160°C/fan 140°C/gas 3.

Make the lime filling by adding the condensed milk to a mixing bowl with the egg, the zest and juice of the limes and then the double cream. Mix until the whole thing is thick, which will take about 30 seconds with an electric hand whisk.

Now put a tablespoon of this filling on to the top of each baked cake, doing your best to keep it fairly even.

Pop a biscuit straight on top of each cake, pressing gently so the lime custard and biscuit meet.

Bake in the oven for 15 minutes. Take out and leave to cool in the tin and then leave to chill in the fridge for at least an hour before eating.

Peel off the cupcake case and then turn each cupcake out onto its biscuity base. I like to serve with a squirt of whippy cream – it's optional but delicious!

# polenta cake
## with rhubarb and rosemary

**Serves** 8–10  **Prep** 25 minutes
**Cook** 35–40 minutes

**For the cake**

220g unsalted butter, softened, plus extra for greasing

220g caster sugar

300g ground almonds

3 large eggs

1 orange, zested and juice reserved in a bowl for later

1 lemon, zested and juice reserved in same bowl as orange juice for later

1 rosemary sprig, leaves removed off the stalk and finely chopped

150g polenta

1 teaspoon baking powder

1 large stick of rhubarb (about 140g), chopped into 2.5cm pieces

100g caster sugar

50g icing sugar

**To serve**

natural Greek yoghurt

When I was a child, my mum would cook rhubarb in curry and I loved it that way, so for a long time I thought of it as savoury. When the school dinner lady plonked some on my plate one day for pudding, I didn't recognize it. But when you are single digits and a tomboy who's desperate to be girly, anything pink is worth a try. It was sloppy and stringy and tart and mainly just weird. After that, I disliked it for years. Hardly selling it, am I? But when it's treated right, rhubarb is delicious, and these days I adore it. Savoury and sweet, it is one of my favourite things about the tail end of summer and the first days of autumn. Picked early, the flesh is perfectly pink! It's beautiful studded in this sweet and fragrant cake, which has a crunchy sugary crust on top.

Start by lightly greasing and lining a 20cm round, loose-bottom cake tin with some baking paper.

Preheat the oven to 180°C/fan 160°C/gas 4.

Add the butter and sugar to a bowl and beat with an electric hand whisk until the mixture is really light and fluffy. Now add the ground almonds and mix well until there are no dry spots.

Add the eggs one at a time, making sure to beat well after each addition.

Now add the orange and lemon zest and the rosemary and mix thoroughly.

In a separate bowl, mix the polenta and the baking powder until they are well combined, then add them to the wet mixture and bring the whole thing together. As soon as you have a glossy yet grainy-looking texture you know it's ready.

Pour the mixture into the prepared tin and smooth to a level surface. Now dot your pieces of rhubarb evenly throughout. Make sure they are standing upright and push them straight in. As the cake bakes it will envelop these little sticks. Pop into the oven and bake for 35–40 minutes.

While it bakes, in a small saucepan mix the caster sugar with the juice from the orange and lemon and place onto a high heat. As soon as the mixture comes to the boil, reduce the heat and leave it to become a thick syrup of about half the volume of liquid you started with. This should take about 10 minutes.

As soon as the cake comes out of the oven, pour the citrus syrup all over it and leave for 5 minutes. Then dust the icing sugar all over the top and leave it to soak into the sugar to form a delicious sugary top.

After about 20 minutes, take the cake out of the tin and pop onto a serving dish.

I love to serve this with simple Greek yoghurt to balance out all those fragrant sweet flavours.

cakes, mini cakes & traybakes

# treacle anise madeleines with grapefruit syllabub

Makes 14–18 (and syllabub serves 5)
Prep 30 minutes   Cook 20 minutes (when baked in two batches)   Best eaten as soon as the chocolate sets or will keep in a tin for 2 days

**For the madeleines**

2 medium eggs

100g soft light brown sugar

1 tablespoon treacle, plus a little extra for decoration, to decorate the syllabub

¼ teaspoon star anise– you can buy this ground or grind a load up yourself

100g plain flour, sifted, plus extra for dusting

1 teaspoon baking powder

100g unsalted butter, melted and cooled, plus extra for greasing tin

150g dark chocolate, melted and cooled

**For the syllabub**

300ml double cream

50g caster sugar

zest and juice of ½ a grapefruit

Madeleines used to be my favourite as a kid, when our local Asian supermarket sold them for 89p a bag. Inside each bag, tumbled amongst one another, were these wonderfully scalloped, slightly dimpled golden cakes. I had to stop myself eating the whole bag in one sitting, but when you're one of six kids, you do have to move fast! Madeleines are so simple to make and my version is sweet and treacly, darker in colour than the classic ones, with a tiny edge dipped in chocolate, and I also make a zesty grapefruit syllabub to dip them into.

Start by making the madeleine mixture. Add the eggs, sugar and treacle to a bowl and whisk until the mixture is light and fluffy. This should take 5 minutes using an electric hand whisk.

Now add the star anise, flour, baking powder and melted butter and mix through till you have a smooth cake batter. Set this aside and leave for 20 minutes, uncovered.

Meanwhile you can be getting on with the syllabub. Add the cream and sugar to a bowl and whisk until the cream begins to thicken.

Now add the zest and juice of ½ a grapefruit and whisk until the cream comes to stiff peaks. Transfer into a serving dish, cover and now the syllabub can go in the fridge until you're ready to eat.

→

Now preheat the oven to 200°C/fan 180°C/gas 6.

Grease the inside of a 12-hole madeleine tray, lightly flour and tip out any excess. You want to make sure all the little grooves are covered – this will just ensure the cakes pop right out of the mould.

If you don't have a madeleine mould, you can use the inside of a shallow fairy cake/jam tart tin, greasing and flouring the same way, or you could use mini tartlet tins, again greasing and flouring as before.

Drop just enough mixture into the cavity so it is about ½cm shy of the top.

Repeat this with all 12 and bake in the oven for 8–10 minutes, until you have a little dimple that's risen on top and they are a medium golden brown.

As soon as they are out of the oven, leave them in the tray for 10 minutes. With the leftover batter, keep making more until you have no mixture left.

Leave them to cool, which shouldn't take long.

Have ready a sheet of baking paper large enough to place all the madeleines on.

When they have cooled, dip a corner at an angle encasing just a third of the madeline into the melted chocolate, and pop onto the baking paper for the chocolate to set. Repeat with the rest.

Serve the madeleines alongside the chilled syllabub, giving it a drizzle of some extra treacle before eating!

# covered-all-over lamington cake

| Serves 10–12 **Prep** 45 minutes, plus cooling and setting **Cook** 1 hour 10 minutes **Keeps for** 2 days |

### For the sponge

285g plain flour, sifted

300g caster sugar

1 tbsp baking powder

1 teaspoon salt

120ml vegetable oil

7 medium egg yolks

180ml water

2 teaspoons lemon extract

7 medium egg whites

½ teaspoon cream of tartar

1 x 300g jar of seedless raspberry jam

250g desiccated coconut

### For the filling

200g unsalted butter, softened

400g icing sugar, sieved

2 tablespoons whole milk

1 teaspoon vanilla extract

200g marshmallows

I've never actually eaten a true Australian lamington, but I have had those fraudulent ones you get packed in a plastic tray. I was shocked to find they only had jam and coconut on the top, when I know for a fact that a proper lamington should be covered all over! So I've taken things into my own hands and created a cake version: light chiffon sponge, smothered in jam, coated in desiccated coconut and filled to the brim with marshmallow buttercream. There you have it: a lamington, not in teeny-weeny squares, but ready to cut into wedges just the way I like, and covered, properly covered!

Begin by washing then thoroughly drying a 25cm round cake tin, about 10cm deep. It's important to remove all traces of grease so the cake can climb up the tin, rather than slide off. It feels counter-intuitive when baking, but it's a must.

Preheat the oven to 170°C/fan 150°C/gas 3 ½.

Add the flour, sugar, baking powder and salt to a bowl and mix well.

Make a well in the centre and add the oil, egg yolks, water and lemon extract. Pop to one side.

Put the egg whites and cream of tartar in another bowl and, using a hand-held whisk, whisk till the mixture comes to stiff peaks.

Now, with the same whisk or beaters, whisk the flour and egg yolk mixture till you have a smooth batter.

Add one third of the egg white mixture to the batter and mix to loosen, using a metal spoon so you don't destroy all those air bubbles.

Now add the rest of the egg white mixture and fold through till you have a light, even, non-streaky cake batter.

Pour into the tin and bake for 55 minutes until golden and firm on top.

→

Meanwhile you can be making your buttercream by adding the butter and icing sugar to a bowl along with the milk and vanilla and whisking till smooth.

Now pop your marshmallows into a microwave-safe bowl and microwave for 30 seconds, till the marshmallows are puffy and doubled in size. This can take longer depending on the power of your micro-wave, so keep zapping in 5-second intervals till they are puffy, then take them straight out.

Add to the buttercream mixture straight away and whisk till well combined. Pop into a piping bag and set aside.

Once the cake is done, take it out of the oven and turn it upside down onto a cooling rack. Leave till the cake has cooled a bit. Once the tin is cool enough to hold, pop it off and leave the cake to cool completely.

Meanwhile, warm the jam till it is liquid – you can do this in a pan or in the microwave.

Spread the coconut in an even layer on a large baking tray and bake in the oven for 12–15 minutes at 180°C/fan 160°C/gas 4, keeping an eye on it all the time and stirring occasionally, till the coconut is a light golden colour. Take out and leave to cool on the tray.

Spread the sides of the cooled cake generously with the jam. With one hand on the top and one on the base, lift the jammy cake and roll it in the tray of coconut – this cake is sturdier than you'd think so get

it into that coconut, turning the whole time till all the sides are covered generously. Press the coconut into the jam, so it really glues itself on.

Now spread a layer of jam onto the top and sprinkle over a generous coating of coconut. Pop a tray on top, put your hand under the cake and flip it over.

You will need to get the dustpan and brush out is all I'm saying; there is no neat way of doing this!

There should be just the top side left to cover, so repeat the process with the jam and coconut, then pop the whole thing onto your chosen serving plate.

Leave for 30 minutes to let the jam dry and the coconut stick firmly.

Use a long, serrated knife to cut horizontally through the cake so you have two rounds, then pop the top one onto a tray.

Pipe the delicious marshmallow buttercream into the exposed cake centre, pop the other round on top and you are good to go.

# drenched rose cake

Serves 8   Prep 30 minutes, plus cooling
Cook 35 minutes   Keeps in an airtight
container for 3–4 days

**For the cake**

200g unsalted butter, softened, plus extra for greasing

200g caster sugar

4 medium eggs, lightly beaten

200g plain flour, sifted

40g pistachios, crushed to a fine powder

**For the syrup**

200g golden syrup

100ml water

3 cardamom pods, seeds crushed

2 tablespoons rose syrup or 1 teaspoon rose extract

1 heaped tablespoon dried rose petals

vanilla ice cream, to serve (optional)

This is my take on a traditional Indian dessert called gulab jamun, in which balls of dough are fried to the point of almost being burnt and then soaked in syrup. I've recreated the idea in cake form. My cake is deliberately over-baked (though not burnt!) to produce a deep-golden exterior with a delicious flavour, in contrast to the simple butter sponge inside. There's a hidden layer of pistachio running through the centre and finally – as the name suggests – the cake is literally drenched in a sweet, sticky, cardamom and rose-infused syrup.

Start by preheating the oven to 200°C/fan 180°C/ gas 6 and generously greasing a 25cm pie dish.

To make the cake batter, add the butter and sugar to a large mixing bowl and whisk until the mixture is really light and fluffy and very pale in colour – it should almost be white. Now add the eggs a little at a time till everything is well combined.

Tip in the flour (we're using no raising agents, because we want a dense cake, with very little rise) and mix until you have a smooth batter.

Pour half the mixture into the prepared dish and level off.

Sprinkle the crushed pistachios over the surface of the batter, leaving a 2.5cm gap around the edge. Gently press the nuts in with the back of a spoon. Then spoon the rest of the batter gently over the top and use a spatula or the back of a spoon to smooth it, making sure all the nuts are covered.

Pop into the oven for 35 minutes. This is the only time you don't have to worry about burning your cake! We want it to catch a little, especially around the edges.

Make the syrup by adding the golden syrup, water, crushed cardamom seeds and rose syrup/extract to a pan over a high heat and bringing the mixture to the boil. As soon as it does, take it off the heat and add the rose petals to rehydrate.

As soon as the cake is done, take it out of the oven and cut it into eight wedges while it is still hot. Pour the syrup all over, concentrating especially on where you made those cuts, so all that delicious syrup can seep in. Leave to cool for about 30 minutes.

I love to eat this while it's still warm, with a big scoop of vanilla ice cream. Take a wedge and give it a go!

# fudgy flapjacky fudge

| | |
|---|---|
| **Makes** 36 pieces | **Prep** 30 minutes, plus cooling |
| **Cook** 15 minutes | **Store** in an airtight jar |

butter for greasing

150g porridge oats

1 teaspoon ground cinnamon

50g currants

115g unsalted butter, softened

450g soft brown sugar

150ml whole milk

397g can of condensed milk

a pinch of salt

As you can see by the title of this recipe, I couldn't decide exactly what this is, so I will let you choose. I love flapjacks and I have a ritual that every time I put petrol in the car (which isn't often, because I seem to like the thrill of running on empty while calculating whether I can make it to the next petrol station – and it's always touch and go!) I always buy one of those flapjacks with a layer of yoghurt on top. But even with the topping, they are just never sweet enough for me. I also love fudge but that can be toe-curlingly sweet. So, in my search for a middle ground, I decided to combine the two. Call it what you will, it's pretty yummy!

Start by adding the oats to a pan over a medium heat and lightly toasting them. Keep stirring as you go and they will eventually become a golden brown – this can take 5–10 minutes.

Remove from the heat, add the ground cinnamon and currants and mix, then put to one side till later.

Lightly grease and line the base and sides of a 20cm square tin with paper. Next, add the butter, sugar, milk, condensed milk and a pinch of salt to a large non-stick pan. Place on a medium heat and stir constantly until the sugar has dissolved. Now bring to the boil, making sure to stir to stop it burning or sticking on the base.

Turn the heat down and simmer the whole mixture, stirring all the time, for 10–15 minutes. The mixture will begin to thicken and the bubbling on the surface will look a little slower. There are a few ways of working out when the mixture is hot enough to set: have an ice-cold bowl of water beside you and drop a little of the mixture in. If it forms into a ball it is ready.

Another way of testing is to use a traditional sugar thermometer, which has the temperatures and stages labelled on the side. The one you're looking for here is the 'soft ball' stage. The most accurate method is to use a digital thermometer, and the temperature you need is between 115 and 118°C.

Keep mixing and, as soon as it's ready, take it off the heat, add the oat mixture immediately and mix it all together really well. Keep mixing to cool and thicken it – this is the most strenuous bit – and you will know it is ready when your arms begin to hurt and the mixture is tighter and tougher to mix. It should start coming away from the sides of the pan. When it does, spoon the mixture into the prepared tin and use the back of a spoon to smooth and press it out evenly.

Leave to cool completely before cutting into small, 3cm squares. As they cool they will harden up. These store really well in an airtight jar. Flapjack or fudge or both: you decide!

# chapter two

# NO-BAKE BAKES

# banana ice cream cheesecake with blueberry compote

**For the base**

160g porridge oats

160g roasted whole hazelnuts

60ml coconut oil, plus extra for greasing the tin

185g golden syrup

a pinch of salt

**For the filling**

7 bananas, chopped and frozen, about 580g

2 tablespoons golden syrup

½ teaspoon ground cinnamon

1 tablespoon cocoa powder

**For the compote**

250g fresh or frozen blueberries

½ lemon, zest and juice

100g caster sugar

---

**Serves** 8–12  **Prep** 30 minutes, plus chilling and freezing  **Cook** 15 minutes

---

Cheesecake in any form is a winner for me and this is a simple no-bake ice cream version, which also happens to be vegan. Its sweet, oaty, hazelnutty base is filled with a banana ice cream 'cheesecake' layer, then topped with a warm blueberry compote.

Start by lining and lightly greasing the base and sides of a 20cm round loose-bottom tin, 7.5cm deep.

Make the base of the cheesecake by toasting the oats and the hazelnuts in a large frying pan on a medium heat for about 5 minutes until they just start to turn a golden brown, making sure to stir all the time to keep the oats moving. Pop them straight into a food processor and blitz to a fine crumb.

Now add the coconut oil and the golden syrup and blitz again till it all clumps together.

Throw the mixture into the prepped tin and, using the back of a spoon, press into the base and 2.5cm of the sides. Leave the base to chill while you make the filling.

Make the topping by taking out the frozen chopped bananas and adding to a food processor with the golden syrup, cinnamon and cocoa. As tempted as you might be to begin whizzing, walk away for 5 minutes and allow the bananas to defrost just very slightly so that they process more easily, then blitz till you have what looks like a soft-scoop ice cream.

Quickly spoon the mixture on top of the prepped base and pop into the freezer till you are ready to eat.

When you are ready to eat, make the compote by adding the blueberries, lemon zest and juice and sugar to a pan and stirring over a medium heat till the blueberries have just softened. This should only take a few minutes. You can make the compote well in advance and, if you do, keep it chilled in the fridge until serving.

Take the cheesecake out of the freezer, slide it out of the cake tin and put it onto your serving dish. Add the warm compote on top and leave for just a few minutes before slicing and enjoying.

# blueberry shinni cake

**Serves** 20    **Prep** 25 minutes, plus chilling
**Cook** 10 minutes

flavourless oil or cake release, for greasing the tin

50g dried blueberries

500g plain flour

1 teaspoon ground cinnamon

1 teaspoon ground green cardamom, ready milled or mill yourself

½ teaspoon salt

250g unsalted butter, chopped into cubes

500ml boiling water

250g caster sugar

75g white chocolate, melted

Shinni is a Bengali spiced flour dough that is served during celebrations and tough times too. Nobody ever really makes it 'just because', so I think that's the reason why I like making it 'just because' – for no particular reason besides a craving for something delicious. It's often served hot, ready for adults and children alike to pinch off warm mounds of the stuff from one large serving dish. But I quite enjoy it cooled, so I've come up with a way to serve it in exactly that fashion, cooked and cooled in a ring mould with a hidden surprise of dried blueberries that adorn the top when turned out, then drizzled with melted white chocolate.

Have a 25cm ring mould (or just a springform cake tin) at the ready and grease well, or use a silicone cake pan. Add the blueberries into the base.

Toast the flour in a non-stick large wok or pan for 10 minutes on a medium heat till golden brown. It's hard to see the change, so compare it to a bag of untoasted flour so you can see. Take off the heat and add the cinnamon, cardamom and salt and stir through.

Add the butter, pop the pan back on the heat and stir till you have a greasy flour and all the butter chunks are melted.

Measure out 500ml of boiling water into a jug, add the sugar and stir till it is dissolved. Make a well in the centre of the flour mixture and pour the hot sugary mix into the centre. Using a whisk, bring the mixture together till you have a dough too tough to mix any more.

Take two spoons and add the dough to the ring mould on top of the blueberries, making sure to keep them where they are. Do this all the way around till you have filled the ring mould.

Pat and pack it all in, then leave to cool. When just slightly warm, refrigerate for at least an hour.

Turn out and drizzle all over with the melted white chocolate, then slice and eat.

# tropical no-bake cookie tray cake

**Serves** up to 9   **Prep** 20 minutes

400g Bourbon biscuits

250ml whole milk

700g jar of tropical fruit in juice, drained

1 lime, zest only

a small handful of fresh mint

600ml double cream

2 teaspoons almond extract

5 tablespoons icing sugar

20g toasted sliced almonds

This is the cheat of all cheats, with no actual baking involved, just a little bit of buying and putting together. It consists of biscuits (chocolate Bourbons, of course), soaked in milk, topped with almond cream and adorned with tropical fruit out of a jar, then finished with the zing of some lime and mint, an extra helping of crushed biscuits and a scattering of toasted sliced almonds.

Have a 20 x 30cm rectangular dish at the ready. I use a glass dish just because I like to see up the sides and all that's going on, but I'm nosey, so use what you have.

Line the base with the Bourbon biscuits. You may need to break off bits of biscuit to fill the little spaces that don't quite take whole Bourbons. Just do this till you have the base covered, saving any that are left over to crumble over the top.

Gently pour all your milk over the biscuits and allow them to soften.

Now place the tropical fruit in a bowl. Add the lime zest and mint and mix through.

Put the cream in a bowl with the almond extract and icing sugar and whip till the mixture comes to stiff peaks. Add to the top of the soaked biscuits and spread over evenly. Scatter the fruity mix all over.

Place the remainder of the biscuits in a bag and crush till you have uneven crumbs. Scatter all over along with the toasted almonds.

Pop in the fridge till you are ready to eat it.

# strawberry and tarragon charlotte
## with passion fruit

butter, for greasing
the tin

275g Madeira cake,
ready-made or
home-made

150g white chocolate,
melted

8 passion fruit, to serve

**For the bavarois cream**

400ml single cream

100g caster sugar

6 medium egg yolks

6 leaves of gelatine
(10g)

360g fresh or frozen
strawberries

a large handful of
fresh tarragon

> **Serves** 8–10    **Prep** 35 minutes, plus chilling
> **Cook** 15 minutes

I learned to make this many, many years ago. It has a bavarois cream in the middle, which is basically a custard set with gelatine, that you can flavour with your choice of fruit purée and set in any sort of mould. I like mine encased in a cake dough, set, sliced and served with passion fruit.

Line a 900g loaf tin with clingfilm. Grease the inside first and then line with a layer of clingfilm so the base and sides are covered, leaving some overhang.

Start by making the cake casing. Crumble the cake into a bowl till you have a fine crumb. Add the melted chocolate to the mixture and get your hands in till the mixture holds together when squeezed. Pop the mixture into the tin and, using your hands and the back of a spoon, press into the base of the tin and push the mixture up the sides, leaving a 2cm gap from the top. Put in the fridge and leave to chill while you make the bavarois.

For the bavarois, pour the cream into a pan and bring to the boil. As soon as it does, take it off the heat.

Whisk together the sugar and egg yolks. Pour into the hot cream slowly, then pour the mixture back into the pan and gently cook, stirring with a spatula, for 5 minutes on a medium heat till the mixture comes up to 80°C. Strain through a sieve to remove any lumps.

Dunk your gelatine leaves into a bowl of cold water till they are fully immersed. Leave for 10–15 minutes and then grab them out, squeeze out any extra water, add to the custard mix and stir.

Blend the strawberries with the tarragon till they are mushed and strain through the same sieve into the hot custard mix. Get rid of the pulp and mix the smooth strawberry and tarragon into the custard.

Pour into the tin over the chilled cake lining and leave to chill in the fridge for up to 4 hours or overnight till completely set. When you are ready to eat, take the pulp out of the passion fruit and serve with the sliced charlotte.

# caramel crunch rocky road

butter, for greasing tin

8 x 52g caramel-filled chocolates, ideally ones with biscuit in

150g dark chocolate, chopped or chips

50g unsalted butter

45g golden syrup

70g breadsticks, lightly broken

150g pistachios, roughly chopped

a good pinch of sea salt flakes

**For the white layer**

150g white chocolate, chopped or chips

50g unsalted butter

45g golden syrup

65g dried cherries and berries

65g dried apricots, chopped

Makes 12 squares    Prep 30 minutes, plus chilling    Cook 2 minutes

There are few rules where rocky road is concerned, but it must be chewy, crunchy and gooey and, of course, contain lots of chocolate. This recipe has all of that and layers too! A gooey layer of chocolate-caramel sweets and melted chocolate mixed with breadsticks for a super-crispy crunch, then a layer of bright salted pistachios and finally a layer of sweet white chocolate mixed with chopped apricots and berries. All set and sliced and ready to indulge.

Begin by lining and lightly greasing an 18 x 25cm rectangular cake tin or a 20cm square cake tin.

Take the chocolates out of their packets and line them up on the base of the tin till you have no more spaces. It's okay to have some gaps as when you put on the next layer it seeps through to hold it all together.

Add the dark chocolate, butter and golden syrup to a microwaveable bowl and heat for 1 minute. Take out and mix till you have a smooth mixture. Leave to cool

for 10 minutes. Add the breadsticks to the mixture and mix through till well coated. Spread out evenly on top of the chocolates.

Now, sprinkle over the chopped pistachios until the base is covered all over. Use the back of a spoon to pat the mixture down and sprinkle over the sea salt flakes. Pop in the fridge for 30 minutes to set a little.

Make the white layer by putting the white chocolate, butter and golden syrup in a microwaveable bowl and melting in the microwave for 1 minute. Take out and stir till smooth. If it looks like it is starting to separate, add a little hot water one spoonful at a time, mixing after each addition till it comes back together and is smooth and glossy.

Add the cherries and berries and chopped apricots and mix through.

Take the tin out of the fridge and add the white layer, making sure to spread evenly, then pop back into the fridge to set for at least a few hours.

Take out and slice, then refrigerate until ready to eat.

# scotch
# creme eggs

Serves 12   Prep 20 minutes, plus chilling

6 creme eggs

90g oaty biscuits

**For the cakey coating**

300g Madeira cake,
   ready-made or
   home-made

1 lemon, zest only

3 tablespoons unsalted
   butter, softened

2 tablespoons icing
   sugar, sieved

1 teaspoon whole milk

My husband and children love creme eggs, so I thought why not make something a little bit special with these to surprise them. I'm not usually a fan, but it turns out I can eat a creme egg happily when it's covered with zesty cake and coated in crumbs!

Start by removing the foil around the eggs, then put all six onto a plate and into the fridge.

Put the biscuits into a freezer bag, seal and crush using a rolling pin, or use a food processor, till you have really fine crumbs, then tip into a bowl.

Now for the cakey outer jacket. Take the cake and break the pieces into a bowl. Using your fingertips or a food processor, break up the cake till you have fine crumbs. Add the lemon zest.

Mix the butter, icing sugar and milk together to get a smooth buttercream. Add a spoon of cake crumbs at a time and mix using your hands so that you get a mixture that clumps together. Keep adding until it is easily mouldable.

Divide the mixture into six and take the eggs out of the fridge. Take each cake mound and flatten in the palm of your hands. Add an egg in the centre and use your hands to mould the cake around the creme egg, really packing the cake around it.

Add each mound to the bowl of biscuit crumbs and roll around till the crumbs coat the cake mixture.

Leave in the fridge till you are ready to eat. I like to leave them to chill and then they're easier to cut in half. A half goes a very long way!

# chewy chocolate krispy squares

Makes 16    Prep 15 minutes plus setting
Cook 10 minutes

120g unsalted butter, plus extra for greasing the tin

6 x 40g nougat caramel chocolate bars, 4 chopped and 2 thinly sliced

70g golden syrup

¼ teaspoon salt

300g puffed rice cereal

250g milk chocolate, melted

These are like the chocolate rice crispy cakes we used to make at school. The kind that ended up in your mouth before they could even make it into the flimsy paper cases. These are delicious and chewy because they are made with chocolate bars already loaded with caramel and nougat. Sometimes simple and nostalgic is just what you need.

Start by lining the base and sides of a 20cm square tin with baking paper, making sure you have some overhang, then lightly grease.

Put the butter, chopped chocolate bars, golden syrup and salt into a large heatproof bowl.

Pop on a pan part-filled with some water. Bring the water to the boil and reduce the heat. Put the bowl over the pan, making sure it sits comfortably without touching the water.

Gently mix till everything has melted and is an even, viscous layer. You may find you need to stir constantly to stop the mixture sticking to the bottom of the bowl. Take off the heat.

Add the puffed rice cereal to a large bowl with lots of room to mix and pour the chocolatey mixture right on top. Stir until every bit of cereal is totally coated.

Dump the lot into the lined tin and use the back of a greased spoon to level off the top.

Take the melted chocolate and spread it over in an even layer. Place your slices of chocolate bar all over and leave the chocolate to set in the fridge.

Cut into squares and you are ready to eat. Welcome to your childhood, but just less messy!

# mango and black peppercorn cranachan

85g unsalted butter

100g cornflakes

1 teaspoon ground black peppercorns

450g tin of mango pulp

1 small mango, peeled and chopped

600ml double cream

3 tablespoons caster sugar

1 tablespoon icing sugar

Makes 6   Prep 20 minutes   Cook 5 minutes

I love simple creamy desserts like this, which are easy to make, easy to adapt and can be prepared in advance. This is my slightly unorthodox take on a classic Scottish recipe, which traditionally contains cream, raspberries and oats, but in my version the soft cream is swirled with mango and buttery cornflakes, with a hint of black peppercorns.

Start by cooking up those cornflakes. Add the butter to a large non-stick pan and as soon as the butter is melted and hot, add the cornflakes.

Toast the cornflakes for about 5 minutes till they are golden and have soaked up the butter. They need to be very crisp, toasty and noisy, so just keep stirring and moving them around.

Pop onto a baking sheet, sprinkle over the black pepper and, using a spoon, toss them around so they all get a little bit of that black pepper. Leave to cool.

Add the mango pulp to a bowl with the mango pieces, mix and leave to one side.

Have six serving dishes at the ready and spoon a layer of the mango mixture into the base of each.

Add the cream to a bowl with the caster sugar and whip to soft peaks. Now add a third of the cooled cornflakes and fold through. Add the mango mixture, leaving just a little for the tops of all six, then ripple the mango through. Add to the six dishes on top of the mango base.

Spoon the remaining mango on top. If you are ready to eat, add the leftover cornflakes; if not, chill and leave the flakes in an airtight pot till you are good and ready.

Serve the desserts with their crunchy top and dusted with a sprinkling of icing sugar.

→

# summer fruit tea-ramisu

200g white chocolate, roughly chopped

100ml hot water

400ml boiling water

6 English breakfast teabags

3 tablespoons caster sugar

1 lemon, zest and juice

175g sponge fingers

350g frozen summer berries, defrosted and drained of any excess liquid

50g white chocolate, grated

**For the creamy filling**

4 medium eggs

100g caster sugar

1 teaspoon vanilla bean extract

a pinch of salt

750g mascarpone

| Serves 12 | Prep 40 minutes |
| --- | --- |

This is a tiramisu but — as the name suggests — made with tea, rather than coffee, since that is my hot beverage of choice. (Coffee, to me, just tastes like aeroplane fuel!) So I steep my sponge biscuits in lemon-infused English breakfast tea and liven everything up with a layer of summer fruits.

This is the kind of recipe where you want to make up all the stages first and then assemble in one crack, so let's do that.

To start the tiramisu, add the chocolate to a bowl, pour over the 100ml hot water and mix till you have a smooth mixture. Set aside to cool. That's one bit done.

Meanwhile, prep the tea by adding the 400ml boiling water to a jug with the teabags and sugar. Leave the teabags in for 5 minutes, then squeeze out as much of that delicious darkness as possible. Take out the teabags and add the juice and zest of the lemon. Set this aside too.

Now to make the creamy filling. I like to go back to basics and do this with a whisk, which allows more control and stops the mascarpone from being over-beaten. Separate the eggs and add the yolks to a bowl with the caster sugar and vanilla.

Put the whites into another clean bowl. Whisk the egg whites first with the pinch of salt till you have stiff peaks that hold.

Using the same whisk, go straight into the egg yolk bowl and whisk till you have a smooth, creamy mixture that is light and pale.

Now place the mascarpone in a smaller bowl and give it a quick mix to make it viscous and easier to mix in. Add the mascarpone to the egg yolk mixture and whisk till combined, then gently fold in the egg whites. Now you have all your elements ready to go.

Have a deep rectangular dish (about 35 x 20cm and 2.7 litres) at the ready.

Take a biscuit and gently dunk it into the tea until it is fully immersed and soaked all over, then put it in the base of the dish. Do this one at a time till you have covered the entire base of the dish with soaked sponge fingers.

Take the chocolate mixture, pour half of it over the soaked biscuits and spread evenly. Take one half of the summer fruits and sprinkle evenly all over the chocolate mixture. Now spoon in half of the mascarpone mixture and spread over the berries in an even layer.

Add another layer of the sponge fingers, dipping them one at a time into the tea till you have done all of them. Spread over the rest of the white chocolate mix and even the layer out. Add the rest of the summer fruits, then evenly spread over the rest of the cream mixture.

Sprinkle over the grated chocolate and pop into the fridge overnight before serving. It needs to really set, so it's a perfect dessert to make in advance.

# chocolate orange vegan mousse

**Makes** 6 **Prep** 40 minutes, plus soaking and chilling

**For the mousse**

chickpea water (aquafaba), drained from a 400g tin

100g caster sugar

100g dark chocolate, melted and cooled

1 teaspoon vanilla extract

2 oranges, zest only, keeping the rest for the topping

**For the cream**

150g cashew nuts

1 teaspoon vanilla bean paste

1 teaspoon caster sugar

175–200ml nut milk

**For the topping**

3 oranges (2 from before plus another)

2 large sprigs of fresh thyme

I'm not vegan but I try to reduce my meat and dairy consumption where I can, so I like experimenting with vegan versions of all kinds of recipes. I've discovered some wonderful alternatives, including this mousse, which is made using chickpea water, known as aquafaba. A good vegan recipe should make you forget about the ingredients that are not included because you're too busy enjoying the ones in front of you. Chocolate, orange and a hint of thyme, what's not to love?

Put the cashews in a bowl and pour in boiling water till the nuts are covered. Leave to soak for 1 hour.

For the mousse, put the liquid from the chickpeas in a bowl. This will become the base of your mousse. As with any meringue, ensure the bowl is grease free or it could stop the chickpea water from whisking up.

Using a hand-held or free-standing mixer, whisk for about 8–10 minutes till the mixture is light and fluffy. Now add the sugar a spoonful at a time, allowing it enough time to dissolve after each addition. You need to whisk for longer with each addition of sugar than you would if making meringue with egg whites, but this stuff is amazing because, unlike with egg whites, you can't overdo it, so keep whisking to stiff peaks.

As soon as you can hold the bowl over your head without the whites falling out, add the melted dark chocolate and fold through. Then add the vanilla and orange zest and fold through till you have a smooth mixture. You will lose some volume in your mousse, but that is to be expected. Spoon the mixture into six jam jars or glasses and pop into the fridge.

Drain the nuts and pop into a blender. Add the vanilla, caster sugar and 175ml of nut milk and whizz till you have a smooth, thick, cream-like consistency. Add a splash more milk if it is very thick. Pour straight onto the top of the mousse in all six jars. Pop into the fridge and prep the fruit.

Top and tail the oranges, cut off all the skin and remove each segment. Chop the segments into pieces and mix with the thyme leaves.

When you are ready to eat, serve the mousses with the orange segments on top.

# virgin mojito possets

Makes 6   Prep 25 minutes, plus chilling
Cook 10 minutes

**For the apples**

1 green apple, peeled, cored and diced

1 lime, juice only

a small handful of fresh mint leaves, finely chopped

**For the posset**

600ml double cream

140g caster sugar

5 juicy limes, juice and zest

**For the crunchy apple topping**

1 green apple, grated, excess moisture squeezed out

1 tablespoon coconut oil, melted

½ teaspoon ground ginger

1 teaspoon icing sugar

I drink 'virgin' everything. Mocktails have become very popular with millennials and, while I'm not sure I quite count as a millennial, it feels great to be a part of an 'in' group. I love virgin mojitos with their combination of fresh apple and mint with a hint of citrus, and if I'm feeling like I want a real hit, I occasionally make them with ginger ale instead of lemonade – that is as wild as I get! This recipe takes all those fresh flavours and puts them into a creamy posset.

Start with six ramekins, about 200ml each. Take your diced apple and pop into a bowl with the lime juice. This is for sharpness and will stop the apple from browning too. Add the mint to the bowl and mix. Divide the mixture into the base of each of the ramekins.

Now make the posset by adding the cream to a pan with the sugar and mixing so the sugar dissolves and mixes into the cream. Put the mixture onto a high heat and bring to the boil, stirring occasionally. Lower the heat as soon as it does and leave to simmer for just 3 minutes.

Take off the heat, add the lime juice and zest and stir through. It should start to thicken almost as soon as you add the lime and mix. Gently pour into the ramekins on top of the apples and leave to cool just slightly before popping into the fridge. These need at least 3 hours to set. The apple pieces will float up to the top, but you can't keep a good thing down!

Meanwhile, make the easy crunchy apple topping. Have a large plate ready lined with some greaseproof paper. Mix the grated apple with the coconut oil and spread evenly all over the paper-lined plate. Pop in the microwave for 2 minutes on the highest setting and then for 20-second bursts till you have very crisp, dry grated apple. Between each bout in the microwave give the apple shreds a little stir to move them around and also to check they are crisping up. Once they are crisp, sprinkle over the ground ginger and icing sugar and mix well.

Once your possets are set, crumble over the apple and they are ready to eat.

# strawberry rice pudding fool

**For the rice**

75g basmati rice

200ml cold water

100ml whole milk

1 vanilla pod, seeds removed

50g caster sugar

600ml double cream

**For the strawberry coulis**

450g strawberries, chopping 225g into small cubes

6 cardamom pods, seeds removed

3 limes, zest only

1½ tablespoons icing sugar

> **Serves** 6    **Prep** 20 minutes, plus soaking
> **Cook** 25 minutes

The inspiration for this came a few years ago when we took our kids away to Disneyworld, Florida, and we had a meal sat among make-believe princesses with Marilyn Monroe voices and eyes like Bambi's. Yet all I can remember is the pudding, involving cooked rice, of some variety, lots of whipped cream, and a simple fruit coulis. Ever since then I've wanted to return, not for the princesses but for the dessert, which stayed with me till I finally decided to make it myself. Now, mine could be totally different, but it tastes divine. Crushed rice cooked, cooled and whipped through cream, and then marbled with strawberry coulis, which I've kept chunky, scented with lime zest and cardamom. Yum!

Begin by putting the rice into a bowl or jug. Add the water and milk and leave to soak for just 10 minutes. I use a stick blender, so I like to put the mixture into the tall jug that came with the blender, or you can save on washing up by doing this in your food processor. Once the 10 minutes are up, whizz with the blender or processor in short bursts till the rice has broken up into bits.

Pour the mixture into a small saucepan, add the vanilla seeds and sugar and pop onto a high heat. Bring to the boil, making sure to stir all the time, and, as soon as it comes to the boil, reduce to a very low heat and cook for 20–25 minutes, stirring constantly, until the rice is mostly soft with a little bite to it but no grittiness. As soon as the rice grains are cooked, take off the heat, pop into a bowl and spread out to allow it to cool as fast as possible.

Now on to the coulis. Add the whole strawberries into a bowl along with the cardamom seeds, lime zest and icing sugar and blitz to a smooth, delicious sauce. Add the chopped strawberries, mix and set aside.

When the rice has cooled, add 100ml of the cream and stir in well to loosen. Now pour the rest of the cream into a bowl and whisk till you have soft peaks – this should not take long. Add the rice to the cream and fold through till you have an even mixture.

Add two-thirds of the strawberry mixture in dollops onto the rice and gently fold through to create ripples. Spoon into a large serving dish or four individual dishes and top with the leftover coulis.

**chapter three**

# TARTS

# & PIES

—

# carrot tart

**Serves** 8  **Prep** 30 minutes, plus chilling
**Cook** 50 minutes

### For the base

125g digestive biscuits (or any biscuits except sandwiched)

25g whole hazelnuts

50g unsalted butter, melted

1½ tablespoons golden syrup

a pinch of salt

### For the carrot filling

400g carrots, grated (no need to peel)

1 tablespoon butter

1 tablespoon water

60g caster sugar

a pinch of salt

1 teaspoon ground cinnamon

1 teaspoon whole coriander seeds, crushed

2 eggs

30g unsalted butter

50ml whole milk

### To serve

whipped cream

a handful of chopped hazelnuts

This is my take on a pumpkin pie, but made with carrots because I always have loads sat in the fridge and this is a great way to use them up. Just like the original, it has a beautiful vibrant orange colour. Spiced with crushed coriander and cinnamon, the filling is baked in a crumbly biscuit and hazelnut base. If you prefer to make this with pumpkin, just swap the main ingredient like for like, though it's best to remove the skin.

Preheat the oven to 180°C/fan 160°C/gas 4 and have a 25cm fluted pie dish at the ready.

Start by making the base. Pop the biscuits into a food processor along with the hazelnuts and blitz to a fine crumb. Now add the melted butter, golden syrup and salt and blitz till you have a mixture that resembles wet sand. Pour out all the mixture into the pie dish.

Using the back of a spoon, push the mixture into the base and sides till you have an even layer all over.

Get a piece of baking paper that will fit inside the biscuit-lined dish and scrunch it up (this just makes it easier to shape around the base and sides). Put on top of the biscuit base and fill with baking beads.

Bake in the oven for 20 minutes.

Meanwhile, start the filling by adding the carrot to a bowl with the butter and water and covering tightly with some clingfilm. Pop into a microwave and cook on the highest setting for 10 minutes. Being careful because the bowl will be very hot, take out and take the clingfilm off, then leave to cool for 10 minutes.

As soon as the base is done, take out of the oven. Lower the oven temperature to 160°C/fan 140°C/gas 3. Remove the paper and baking beads.

Now back to the filling. Put the cooked carrot into the food processor and add the caster sugar, salt, cinnamon and coriander seeds. Blitz smooth, then add the eggs, butter and milk and give it a final whizz.

Pour the mixture straight onto the biscuit base and bake for 30 minutes. If after 20 minutes you find the edges are starting to catch or get dark, pop a piece of foil on top for the rest of the baking time. Once baked, take out of the oven and leave to cool completely. Once it is totally cooled, I recommend chilling it for at least 3 hours before you eat it.

Serve chilled, cut into wedges with a swirl of whipped cream on top and a sprinkling of toasted hazelnuts. It will keep in the fridge for 3 days.

# portuguese custard tarts

**For the tart shells**

375g ready-rolled puff pastry

1 teaspoon ground nutmeg

**For the filling**

155g caster sugar

1 egg

2 egg yolks

1 tablespoon cornflour

1 teaspoon vanilla bean extract

400ml double cream

a pinch of ground nutmeg

**Makes** 12   **Prep** 30 minutes, plus cooling
**Cook** 35 minutes

The first time I ate these was out of a box from the local supermarket. Second time was at a popular chain restaurant. Third time was at a food market in London. They got slightly better each time, but then I had them in Portugal, in the sun, and that's when I really had them. The crisp, buttery tart case is filled with a set custard with just a kiss of nutmeg. Delicious! Easy to eat, but really easy to make too, especially if you want to get close to the real thing.

Start by sorting the pastry. Roll the pastry out and sprinkle the dough evenly with the nutmeg.

Now re-roll the pastry like you would a Swiss roll, starting with the long edge, until the whole thing is fully rolled up. Cut into 12 equal pieces.

Have a 12-hole muffin tin at the ready. Pop each round of pastry into one of the cups of the tin, with the swirly side up so you can see the swirls of nutmeg.

Dampen your hands slightly so the pastry doesn't stick and, using your thumbs, gently push the pastry from the centre out so the dough evenly covers the base and sides of each cup. Pop into the fridge while you make the custard.

Start on the custard by adding the sugar, egg, egg yolks, cornflour and vanilla into a bowl and whisk till combined.

Put the cream into a pan and just bring to the boil. As soon as it comes up to the boil, take off the heat. Gently pour the hot cream in a very steady stream into the eggy mixture.

Pour it all back into the pan and heat gently, stirring all the time till the mixture has thickened. As soon as it does, take off the heat. Leave to cool for 30 minutes.

Preheat the oven to 200°C/fan 180°C/gas 6.

Take the pastry out of the fridge and pour the custard mixture into the pastry, leaving a slight gap on top just to make sure they are not overfilled. Sprinkle a dusting of nutmeg on the top of each one.

Pop into the oven and bake for 20–25 minutes. The custard filling will puff up over the edges, but don't worry, because as soon as they come out of the oven and begin to cool, they come right back down.

I would leave these for about 30 minutes so the custard is fully set before eating. However, they are equally delicious chilled out of the fridge. It all depends on your patience and/or desperation!

# grapefruit ganache tart

Serves 8-10
**Prep** 45 minutes, plus chilling **Cook** 35 minutes

### For the chocolate pastry

160g plain flour, plus extra for dusting

20g cocoa powder

40g icing sugar

a pinch of fine sea salt

110g cold butter, cubed

1 medium egg yolk

### For the filling

300g white chocolate, chopped or chips

200ml double cream

1 grapefruit, zest only (saving the juice for the sauce)

### For the sauce

juice of 1 grapefruit (approx. 200ml)

75g caster sugar

50g unsalted butter

1 teaspoon cornflour

This has all the qualities of a great tart plus some bonus features. The short, crumbly, pastry base contains cocoa, which makes it a beautiful dark colour. The rich, velvety ganache filling is offset with a hint of grapefruit. It's served with a zesty grapefruit sauce drizzled all over.

For the pastry, put the dry ingredients in a food processor. Add the butter and blitz till you have a fine breadcrumb-like texture. Add the egg yolk and blitz again till you get clumps gathering and no excess flour. If it is too floury and not coming together, add a few drops of water and whizz till small clumps start to form.

Now tip the dough clumps out and bring together into a nice round mound. Flatten and wrap in clingfilm. Pop into the fridge to chill for 30 minutes.

Meanwhile, preheat the oven to 200°C/fan 180°C/gas 6 and put a baking tray on the middle shelf. Have a 23cm fluted loose-bottomed tin at the ready.

Take out the pastry and on a floured surface roll out to about 35cm diameter – large enough to line the base and sides of the tin with an overhang. Now line the tin

with the pastry, making sure to get it right into the fluted edges. Prick the base with a fork to make holes for steam to escape. Put in the freezer for 15 minutes.

Take out and fill the base with baking paper and baking beads. Blind bake for 15 minutes, then remove the paper and beads, and bake for another 15 minutes. Take out and leave for 10 minutes before carefully cutting off any overhanging pastry.

Leave the tart shell to cool in the tin and start on the filling by adding the chocolate to a heatproof bowl.

Add the cream to a small pan and gently heat. As soon as the cream just comes to the boil, take off the heat and pour straight into the chocolate. Stir until it has all mixed in, the chocolate has melted and the mixture is smooth. Add the zest of the grapefruit and stir through, then pour into the prepared tart shell. Pop into the fridge and leave to chill completely.

Make the sauce by adding the grapefruit juice, sugar, butter and cornflour to a small pan. Pop onto a low to medium heat and mix till you have a mixture that is smooth and thick and coats the back of the spoon. Take off the heat.

Once the tart is chilled, slice, plate, drizzle and enjoy. This will keep in the fridge for 3 days.

# french onion and blue cheese tart

2 tablespoons butter

2 large sprigs of lemon thyme

1 clove of garlic, grated

5 onions, thinly sliced (you will need about 1kg)

1 teaspoon freshly ground black pepper

1 teaspoon salt

2 teaspoons caster sugar

1 sheet of ready-rolled puff pastry

1 egg, lightly beaten

150g blue cheese

a small handful of chopped fresh chives, to serve

**Serves** 8    **Prep** 25 minutes
**Cook** 45 minutes

Given how often we need onions to start a recipe, let's not forget or discount how important they really are. So in this tart I've made them the star of the show, sweet and lightly scented, in pride of place on a layer of light, puffy pastry and delicious crumbled blue cheese.

Start by cooking the onions. They need to be cooked slowly on a low heat, so it's best to begin with those.

Add the butter to a large non-stick frying pan — we have a load of onions to cook. When the butter has melted, pick off the thyme leaves and add, then add the garlic and onions. Mix everything together.

Now add the pepper, salt and sugar and mix. Leave to cook on a medium heat for 30 minutes, stirring occasionally, until you have onions that look like the kind you would only eat with a burger in a Sunday market at 6 a.m.!

Whilst that cooks, start on the pastry. Preheat the oven to 200°C/fan 180°C/gas 6. Line a baking tray with some paper or use the paper the pastry comes in and roll out the pastry on to the tray.

Using a knife, score a smaller rectangle 1cm inside the pastry rectangle, making sure not to cut all the way through. Pierce the inner rectangle with a fork all over to allow the steam to escape when it bakes.

Brush the edges with the egg and bake for 20 minutes until golden all over.

Take out and, using the back of a spoon, push down all the puffed-up pastry of the inner rectangle, leaving you a nice neat border.

Take the blue cheese and crumble all over the inner rectangle of the pastry. Add the onions and scatter them all over till you have an even layer. Now bake for 15 minutes.

Take out and leave to cool for 10 minutes before eating, sprinkled with the chives.

# orange and lemongrass meringue pie

Serves 8    Prep 30 minutes, plus chilling
Cook 10 minutes

## For the base

250g sugar-frosted cornflake cereal

125g unsalted butter, melted

## For the filling

2 large oranges, juice and zest (you will need 200ml juice)

4 sticks of lemongrass

25g cornflour

250g caster sugar

6 large egg yolks

## For the meringue

4 large egg whites

½ teaspoon cream of tartar

255g caster sugar

125ml water

Meringue pie is a classic, especially the familiar lemon variety. But it's also a recipe where there are so many variations possible and this is just one of countless ways to mix it up. Instead of biscuit or pastry I've made the base with sweet crisp cereal and instead of lemon curd I've gone for orange and lemongrass. The only bit that hasn't changed is the top, as I think meringue needs no improvement.

Line the base of a 23cm loose-bottomed tin with a circle of baking parchment.

Pop the frosted flakes into a food processor and blitz to a fine crumb. Add the melted butter and whizz till you have a mixture that resembles wet, clumpy sand. Tip it out into the tin and, using the back of a spoon, cover the base and sides, making sure to pack it all in really tightly. Pop into the fridge to chill and set.

Now for the curd. Add the orange juice and zest to a non-stick pan. Bash the lemongrass to release all the flavours, chop into little pieces and add to the pan.

Add the cornflour, sugar and egg yolks and stir everything together. It will be lumpy and not look great at this point, but pop it onto the hob on the lowest heat and mix till you have a smooth curd that coats the back of a spoon.

Take off the heat and push through a sieve, to remove lumps and extract more of that lemongrass flavour. Leave to cool completely. As soon as it is cool, add to the crispy tart base, level off and pop into the fridge.

For the meringue, put the egg whites and cream of tartar into the bowl of a stand mixer with the whisk attachment.

Mix the sugar and water in a medium saucepan. Heat gently until the sugar has dissolved, then bubble until the syrup reaches 110°C. When that happens, start beating the egg whites in the stand mixer until they reach stiff peaks. Once the syrup reaches 118°C, pour the syrup slowly onto the egg whites with the motor still running at a slow speed.

Once the syrup is mixed in, increase the speed to medium–high and beat for another 3–5 minutes until thick and shiny.

Take the tart shell out of the tin and put on a serving dish. Dollop peaks of meringue onto the curd. The more swirls you have the more beautiful it will look. Grill the top for just long enough to toast or use a blowtorch to colour the meringue.

→

# pecan pie empanadas

**For the pastry**

550g plain flour

1 teaspoon salt

230g unsalted butter

1 medium egg and
1 medium egg yolk,
lightly beaten

140ml cold water

**For the filling**

2 medium eggs

50g light soft brown
sugar

150g unsalted butter,
softened

3 tablespoons plain flour

1 tablespoon whole milk

1 teaspoon vanilla extract

200g pecans, roughly
chopped

227g tub of clotted
cream

1 egg, lightly beaten

vegetable oil, for frying

salt

> **Makes** 26  **Prep** 50 minutes, plus chilling
> **Cook** 40 minutes  **Can be assembled** a
> day in advance and then fried to serve

These are all-to-yourself pecan pies made in individual pastry parcels, so no sharing, just yours, to pick up and enjoy. Delicious crisp pastry is filled with a pecan and brown sugar mixture and, to make them even more delicious, clotted cream, like a built-in topping. As the empanadas fry and the filling warms up, so does the cream.

Start by making the pastry. Add the flour and salt to a bowl and mix. Add the butter and rub in till you have something that resembles breadcrumbs.

Make a well in the centre, add the eggs and mix in. Add the water and mix till you have a dough that comes together in a mound. To make life easier you can do all of the above in a food processor in the same order till you have a dough. Flatten the dough, wrap in clingfilm and chill in the fridge for an hour to firm up.

Make the filling by adding the eggs, sugar, butter, flour, milk, vanilla and pecans into a bowl and mixing till you have an even mixture. Pop to one side.

Take the dough out and roll to about 3mm thick, then cut out 26 circles with a 10cm round cutter.

Spread the circles out on a surface and evenly distribute your filling onto them, making sure to put the filling off-centre, because the other half has to fold over to create a semicircle. Now add a teaspoon of cream right on top of each one.

Brush the unfilled half of each circle with beaten egg and fold over to enclose the filling. Press and seal all the way around the join. Pop them all onto a tray and leave to chill for an hour.

Heat enough oil in a pan to be able to semi-deep shallow fry these. I like to use a large, deep frying pan and add enough oil to get just about halfway up. Heat the oil until, when you add a pinch of bread, it comes up to the surface. If you are using a thermometer, which is the most accurate way, then it needs to be at 180°C.

Add 3–4 empanadas, depending on the size of your pan, and fry for just a few minutes on each side till light golden brown. Each batch will take about 5 minutes. Sprinkle with a little salt as they come out of the oil and drain on kitchen paper. These are best eaten while hot.

# canadian butter tart

**Serves** 8   **Prep** 25 minutes, plus cooling
**Cook** 1 hour

### For the base

500g shortcrust pastry block, chopped into 1cm chunks

30g icing sugar, plus extra for dusting

### For the topping

2 medium eggs

120g soft brown sugar

1 teaspoon almond extract

2 teaspoons espresso powder

1 tablespoon cornflour

50g unsalted butter, melted, plus extra for greasing the tin

a pinch of salt

50ml whole milk

50g walnuts, roughly chopped

100g raisins or currants

This was a must-try item on my list of 'things to eat' when we visited Canada one summer. Every bit of research I did told me to go and find these. They are sweet, crunchy with nuts and crumbly with pastry. What I loved most about them was the pastry, as I always like more of it rather than less. So my version of the recipe has lots of chunky pastry pieces on the base, and just a little of the sweetness with the buttery, nutty topping, plus raisins and a hint of coffee.

Preheat the oven to 200°C/fan 180°C/gas 6. Grease and line the base and sides of a 18 x 27cm brownie tin. Make sure to grease the inside on top of the paper lightly too.

Take your chunks of pastry, pop them into a bowl and sprinkle over all of the icing sugar. Toss around to make sure they are evenly coated with the icing sugar. Tip the pieces into the prepared tin in an even layer and sprinkle in any leftover icing sugar. Bake in the oven for 45 minutes.

Meanwhile, make the topping by adding the eggs, sugar, almond extract, espresso and cornflour to a small non-stick saucepan and give it all a really good mix. Add the butter, salt and milk and whisk through till well combined.

Pop onto a medium heat and keep whisking, heating the mixture till it becomes thicker. This should take 5 minutes. As soon as it has thickened, take off the heat, add the walnuts and raisins or currants and mix through.

Take the pastry base out of the oven and top with the sweet butter mixture in an even layer. Pop back into the oven for 15 minutes. It will begin to bubble on the edges. Take out and leave to cool in the tin for 10 minutes.

Lift out and leave on the paper on a cooling rack till totally cooled down. Cut out squares and dust with a little icing sugar before serving.

# potato rösti quiche

Serves 6   Prep 30 minutes, plus cooling
Cook 50 minutes

**For the base**

butter or oil, for greasing the tin

1 large white potato, unpeeled (you should have 325g)

1 large sweet potato, unpeeled (you should have about 325g)

1 teaspoon salt

1 teaspoon paprika

1 teaspoon garlic granules

3 teaspoons onion granules

40g plain flour

1 medium egg, plus another for brushing

**For the filling**

3 medium eggs

150ml whole milk

150g mature Cheddar cheese, grated

a small handful of fresh chives

salt and pepper

This re-imagined quiche is all about the base! Made from different coloured potatoes, grated and pressed into a tin, it's filled with a creamy cheese and chive mixture. Delicious and also super simple.

Preheat the oven to 180°C/fan 160°C/gas 4. Start by generously greasing a 24cm round tart tin or pie dish, preferably not loose-bottomed as this will save us from any leakages.

Grate the potatoes and squeeze out any excess moisture. Pop the potato into a bowl along with the salt, paprika, garlic, onion and flour and mix really well, making sure it is all evenly distributed. Add the egg and mix through well – you should have a mixture that is well coated and clumps together.

Tip the mixture out into the dish and using the back of a spoon press tightly into the base and sides. Bake for 25–30 minutes.

Take the dish out and using the back of a spoon press the mixture into the base and sides again. Brush the base and sides with the egg, generously filling in any gaps that might be there and any gaps that might not be. More is more! Pop back into the oven for 5 minutes.

Meanwhile, make the filling by adding the eggs and milk to a jug and whisking till well blended.

Take the tart shell out and add the cheese into the shell. Pour the egg and milk mixture straight in, sprinkle over the chives and add a sprinkling of salt and a generous sprinkling of pepper. Bake in the oven for 20 minutes till the centre is just wobbly.

Leave to cool for about 30 minutes, allowing the eggy custard mix to set, then take out, slice and it is ready to eat.

# sfeeha triangle

## For the dough

500g strong bread flour, plus extra for dusting

7g fast-action yeast

1 teaspoon sugar

3 tablespoons olive oil

1 teaspoon salt

300ml warm water

## For the filling

3 tablespoons olive oil

3 cloves of garlic, crushed

100g pine nuts

1 onion, finely chopped

500g lamb mince

1 teaspoon salt

1 teaspoon cayenne pepper

1 tablespoon freshly ground black pepper

½ teaspoon ground cinnamon

1 teaspoon allspice

1 tablespoon honey

a large handful of fresh parsley

## For the dip

10 tablespoons good olive oil

6 tablespoons plain yoghurt

a drizzle of pomegranate molasses

a handful of pomegranate seeds

1 teaspoon za'atar

## For the glaze

50g unsalted butter

a good pinch of salt

1 tablespoon dried parsley

Serves 6-8
Prep 50 minutes, plus proving
Cook 55 minutes

I first ate this while fasting. We'd been to prayer, and afterwards there was food on sale to raise money for charity. So my memories are doubly good, because as well as the wonderful feeling of giving, it's a little bit special when you get to break your fast and enjoy some food. The ones I ate that time were delicious little individual triangles, encasing a sweet, spicy mince filling, but my recipe is for one big triangle to share.

For the dough, add the flour to a large mixing bowl. Add the yeast, sugar and oil to one side and the salt to the other side. Mix everything together and make a well in the centre.

Add the water and mix till you bring the dough together. If you are using a mixer, knead with a dough hook attached, or lightly dust the work surface and knead the dough till it is smooth, pliable and stretchy.

This can take 10 minutes by hand or 5 minutes in a stand mixer. Pop back into the bowl, cover and leave in a warm place to double in size.

Meanwhile, make the filling. Add the oil to a non-stick pan. As soon as the oil is hot, add the garlic and pine nuts and, as soon as both are golden brown, add the onion and stir and cook for 10 minutes till the onion is soft. Add the lamb mince and cook until browned.

Now add the salt, cayenne, black pepper, cinnamon, allspice and honey. Cook for 10 minutes. Take off the heat, add all the parsley and leave to cool completely.

Preheat the oven to 220°C/fan 200°C/gas 7 and line a baking tray with some baking paper.

Once the dough has doubled in size, tip it out and knock out all the air. Roll the dough out to a circle that is about 5mm thin. Lift the dough onto the lined tray.

Tip the mixture for the filling into the centre of the dough in a circle. Now take the dough at three equidistant points and bring right into the centre so

you have a triangle shape. Pinch in the centre, but leave the seams on top exposed so you can see the filling. Pop onto the baking tray and push gently to flatten. Bake for 25 minutes.

To make the dip, add the oil to a bowl and spoon the yoghurt into the centre. Drizzle over the pomegranate molasses, sprinkle on the pomegranate seeds and then the za'atar and it's ready to devour.

Once the triangle is baked and while still hot, brush with the melted butter and sprinkle all over with the salt and dried parsley. Serve with the dip.

# rainbow veg pakora picnic pie

**Serves** 8   **Prep** 1 hour
**Cook** 40 minutes

### For the filling

1 red pepper, diced

1 carrot, grated

1 x 326g tin of sweetcorn (drained weight 285g)

1 small courgette, diced

½ aubergine, diced

½ red onion, diced

a large handful of fresh chives, finely chopped

a large handful of fresh coriander, finely chopped

1 teaspoon salt

2 teaspoons garlic granules

2 teaspoons chilli flakes

2 teaspoons cumin seeds

1 tablespoon curry powder, mild or hot, whatever you prefer

2 medium eggs

100g chickpea or gram flour

### For the pastry

265g plain flour

55g strong bread flour

½ teaspoon salt

2 teaspoons curry powder

135ml water

70g butter

1 egg, lightly beaten

Pies are the thing I find most satisfying to make and that doesn't even include the eating process! An all-in-one meal, in an edible casing, filled with pretty much anything you want (apart from soup! Let's not go there). This one is filled with lightly spiced rainbow veg, encased in a golden brown, curry-flavoured pastry crust. Inspired by a pakora, it has all the colours, all of the flavour, but none of the frying.

Start by making the filling. Add the red pepper, carrot, sweetcorn, courgette, aubergine, onion, chives and coriander into a bowl. Add the salt, garlic, chilli, cumin and curry powder and get in there and mix till everything looks relatively evenly distributed.

Now add the eggs and mix through, then the flour and mix again. Set aside and get on to the pastry.

Preheat the oven to 200°C/fan 180°C/gas 6 and have ready a 25cm round tart tin, 5cm deep and with a loose bottom or fixed base.

To make the pastry, add the flours, salt and curry powder to a bowl, mix and create a small well in the centre.

Add the water to a small pan with the butter and bring to the boil. As soon as the butter has melted, take off the heat and add straight into the dry ingredients.

Mix using the back of a spoon and then as soon as it is cool enough to handle, get your hands in and bring the dough together. When it does, divide the mixture by separating off one third.

Take the bigger bit and roll till you have pastry large enough to cover the base and sides of the tin with a little overhang.

Tip in the vegetable mixture and level off. Take the other bit of dough and roll till you have enough to cover the top. Brush the edge with egg and pop the top on. Cut the edges and then crimp. Cut a hole in the centre for the air to escape. Brush the top with egg. Bake in the oven for 40 minutes.

Take out and leave for at least an hour before eating.

# beetroot tatin
## with mackerel and a dill pesto

> Serves 4    Prep 30 minutes    Cook 40 minutes

**For the tatin**

500g puff pastry block or ready-rolled puff pastry

3 tablespoons oil

400g cooked beetroot, drained, dried and quartered

2 tablespoons balsamic vinegar

2 tablespoons soft brown sugar

1 small orange, zest and juice

**For the pesto**

50g pine nuts, toasted

2 cloves of garlic

100g fresh dill, roughly chopped

50g Parmesan cheese, grated

150ml olive oil

**To serve**

140g hot smoked mackerel, skin removed and flaked

crème fraîche

This is such a simple lunch or dinner and can easily be assembled in advance, ready to bake at a later point. I love beetroot, in particular the sheer purple of the veg, but also that sweet, delicious, earthy flavour, which I adore cooked gently with orange and covered with a flaky puff pastry. I like to serve this tart with flakes of hot smoked mackerel and a dill pesto. If you have pesto left over, store it in a jar covered with a thin layer of oil, then seal the lid and it will keep in the fridge for 1–2 weeks.

Preheat the oven to 200°C/fan 180°C/gas 6. For this recipe you need an oven-safe, round, deep frying pan, about 25cm in diameter.

Roll the pastry into a 29cm circle. Pop onto a tray and leave to chill.

Add the oil to the pan and heat, then add the beetroot and warm through. These are already cooked, so half the work is done for you. Add the balsamic vinegar to the beetroot along with the sugar, orange juice and zest and cook through till the beets are sat in a thick, sticky mixture. This should take about 5 minutes, but be sure not to burn the sugar and keep an eye on that. Take off the heat.

Bring the pastry out of the fridge and gently lay it on top of the beetroot.

Using a spatula or the end of a dinner knife, tuck the edges of the pastry into the pan under the beetroot. Do this all the way around to create a 'cup', which will hold the beetroot once the tart is turned out. Pierce the top of the pastry to allow the steam to escape. Bake in the oven for 35 minutes.

Make the pesto by adding all the ingredients to a blender and whizzing till smooth.

When the tatin is ready, remove from the oven but leave in the pan for 5 minutes before turning out. Turn out and add the flaked mackerel all over the top, then drizzle with the pesto and serve sliced with crème fraîche on the side.

# chicken, brie, cranberry and pink pepper pithivier

2 x 500g blocks of puff pastry

3 tablespoons olive oil

4 cloves of garlic

1 onion

1 teaspoon salt

4 tablespoons pink peppercorns, crushed

300g chicken thighs, cut into cubes

100g dried cranberries

2 egg yolks, lightly beaten

200g Brie cheese

Serves 6    Prep 30 minutes, plus chilling
Cook 50 minutes    Can be assembled up to
1 day in advance and then baked to serve

A French classic, this beautifully scored, round, puff pastry pie can be filled with all manner of ingredients, sweet or savoury. With such a reliable exterior, the inside is all to play for. I've filled mine with chicken that's spiced and sweetened with pink peppercorns and cranberries, around a delicious centre of melted Brie.

Line two baking trays with baking paper.

Take the puff pastry blocks and roll them one by one on a floured surface. Roll to a 5mm thickness and cut using a 25cm round, then cut another circle to a 30cm round. Leave both to chill on a tray while you make the filling.

Now make the filling by adding oil to a non-stick pan. Blitz the garlic and onion to a smooth paste.

Add the paste to the hot oil and cook till the mixture is thick and brown – this should take about 10 minutes over a medium heat. Now add the salt and pepper-corns and mix.

Add the chicken along with the cranberries and mix and cook till you have a dry chicken mix and the chicken is cooked through, which should take around 7 minutes at most. Take off the heat and leave to cool completely.

Take the smaller round and lightly brush the edges with egg yolk.

Carefully slice off the top and base of the Brie, just to make it shorter. Pop the Brie in the centre of the round and then add the chicken all around the edge and over the top of the Brie, patting it into a mound and avoiding the brushed egg yolk edge.

Take the second, larger circle and place on top. Push down over the filling, easing out any air bubbles as you go and sealing all around the edges firmly. Brush the top with the egg yolk and pop into the fridge for 30 minutes.

Preheat the oven to 200°C/fan 180°C/gas 6 and put a tray in the oven to heat up.

Flute the edge using the back of a knife to create a scalloped edge and score the top. Brush the egg yolk again and bake for 25–30 minutes. If the pastry is looking very dark after 20 minutes, cover loosely with foil and reduce the oven temperature to 180°C/fan 160°C/gas 4. Serve straight from the oven.

# tomato galette

**For the pastry**

125g plain flour

100g chickpea flour

a pinch of salt

100g unsalted butter

3–4 tablespoons cold water (may need less or more)

**For the filling**

2 tablespoons vegetable oil

1 clove of garlic, crushed

3 anchovies or ½ teaspoon salt

325g cherry tomatoes, halved

1 teaspoon smoked paprika

1 tablespoon tamarind paste

1 x 198g tin of sweetcorn, drained

4 tablespoons hummus

a small handful of capers

a small handful of fresh basil

**Serves** 4  **Prep** 25 minutes
**Cook** 45 minutes

This is somewhat like a pizza, but with a few differences. It has a base, tomatoes and toppings, but is easier and quicker to make from scratch, while still just as delicious.

Start by making the pastry. Add the flours and salt to a bowl with the butter and rub the butter in till you have a mix that looks like breadcrumbs.

Add the water a tablespoon at a time and mix and squeeze the mixture until it starts to come together. As soon as you have a mound of pastry, bring it together and wrap in clingfilm, flatten and leave in the fridge while you cook the tomatoes.

Add the oil to a pan and, as soon as the oil is hot, add the garlic and anchovies and, using the back of a spoon, push the anchovies and squeeze till they are broken down. This will add seasoning.

Now add the tomatoes along with the paprika and cook on a medium heat for 3–4 minutes until it is just starting to soften slightly. Add the tamarind and sweetcorn and cook through gently for about 10 minutes till the mixture is fairly dry. Take off the heat.

Preheat the oven to 200°C/fan 180°C/gas 6 and pop a baking tray in the oven to heat up.

Roll the pastry out to about 5mm thick on a piece of baking paper – this will just make it easier to move onto the tray later. This does not have to be an even round – being a little rough around the edges will add to the texture.

As soon as you have a rough circle, add the hummus in the centre and spread all over, leaving about 5cm around the edges. Now add all your tomato and sweetcorn mixture on top and bring the edges over to create a 'crust' as such – you can be as rough as you like. If the pastry breaks up at the edges, just pinch it together. This is quite a brittle dough so you may find it cracks as you fold it over. Pinch it back together and it will be just fine.

Place on the heated tray, pop into the oven and bake for 25–30 minutes.

As soon as it is out, roughly chop the capers and rip up the basil and sprinkle all over. Serve sliced into wedges.

# chapter four

# DESSERTS

# tutti-frutti pavlova

**For the meringue**

4 medium egg whites

250g caster sugar

1 teaspoon white vinegar

2 teaspoons cornflour

1 teaspoon vanilla extract

butter, for lightly greasing the tray

**For the tutti-frutti cream**

350ml double cream

3 tablespoons icing sugar

1 tablespoon cornflour

100g glacé cherries, chopped

100g pistachios, roughly chopped

100g mixed peel

**For decoration**

25g dark chocolate shavings

**Serves** 8　**Prep** 25 minutes　**Cook** 1 hour, plus cooling　**Best eaten** straight away but will keep in the fridge for 1 day

My earliest memory of 'tutti-frutti' is of cakes we used to buy at the local Asian supermarket. They came lined up on a tray wrapped in see-through plastic, with all their glorious tutti-frutti on show. They always looked so inviting. Anything with that same delicious colour is a winner for me, so I've laced it through a simple whipped cream that sits happily on a chewy meringue nest.

Preheat the oven to 150°C/fan 130°C/gas 2 and lightly grease a baking tray. Using a pencil, trace around a 25cm plate onto baking paper and then flip it over onto the greased baking tray. Make sure the paper sticks so it doesn't flap in the oven.

For the meringue, add the egg whites to a bowl and whisk until soft peaks start to form, then slowly add the sugar a spoonful at a time, allowing the crystals to melt. As soon as you have used all the sugar and you have stiff peaks, add the vinegar, cornflour and vanilla and whisk one last time to incorporate.

Spoon or pipe the meringue into the circle on the baking paper, as neatly or roughly as you like. Create a slight indent in the centre, where your cream will sit.

Bake in the oven for 1 hour. When the hour is up, turn the oven off and leave the meringue in there until the oven is totally cold.

Pop onto a serving dish or leave in an airtight container till you are ready to serve.

Add the cream to a bowl with the icing sugar and cornflour and whisk until you have soft peaks. Add about half of the chopped cherries, pistachios and mixed peel and gently fold through, reserving the rest for the top.

I like to take two spoons and dollop the cream mixture onto the meringue in a rough fashion. Finally, scatter with the rest of the cherries, pistachios and mixed peel and sprinkle all over with the chocolate shavings.

# roasted fruit cobbler

**Serves** 8   **Prep** 30 minutes   **Cook** 35 minutes
**Best eaten** straight away but will keep in the fridge for 2 days

The fruit layer at the bottom of this cobbler is the sweet and colourful foundation for my unconventional chocolate coconut cobbles. Delicious to look at, delicious to eat, but satisfyingly simple to make, this dessert is a firm favourite in our house.

**For the fruity layer**

melted butter, for brushing the dish

4 plums

4 peaches

50g caster sugar

2 tablespoons cornflour

125g blueberries

1 lemon

a small handful of fresh mint, chopped

**For the cobbles**

150g unsalted butter, softened

150g caster sugar

3 medium eggs

150g self-raising flour

50g desiccated coconut

30g cocoa powder

50g chocolate chips, or roughly chopped chocolate

a sprinkling of salt

**To serve**

ice cream

50g milk chocolate, melted

Start by getting a medium roasting dish, about 25 x 30 x 5cm. Brush the base generously with butter. Preheat the oven to 190°C/fan 170°C/gas 5.

Cut the plums and peaches into quarters, remove the stones and drop the flesh into a large bowl. Sprinkle over the sugar and cornflour and mix through until everything is evenly coated. Pour the mixture into the prepared dish and level off. Sprinkle in the blueberries and zest the lemon on top, making sure you get it all over. Finally, scatter the mint over, pushing the leaves in a little so they don't burn when baked.

Now, make the cobbles by adding the butter to a bowl with the sugar and the eggs and mixing by hand or using an electric mixer. Add the flour, coconut and cocoa powder and mix through until you have a stiff cake batter. Add the choc chips and mix them through.

Take an ice cream scoop or use two tablespoons and dollop the mixture sporadically all over the fruit, leaving little gaps in between.

Sprinkle the cobbles with a little salt and bake in the oven for 35 minutes, until the fruit is soft, the cobbles are crunchy and you are ready to eat this bad boy!

We like to eat this with ice cream and a drizzling of melted milk chocolate.

→

desserts

# brigadeiro with sweet and salty pitta chips

**For the brigadeiro**

2 x 397g tins of
  condensed milk

60g cocoa powder

50g unsalted butter

oil, for greasing the bowl

6 passion fruit

**For the chips**

6 pitta breads, cut
  into strips

150g unsalted butter,
  melted

1 teaspoon sea salt
  flakes

4 tablespoons
  demerara sugar

cocoa powder,
  for dusting (optional)

---

**Serves** 6–8    **Prep** 25 minutes, plus chilling
**Cook** 30 minutes    **Can be assembled** up to
24 hours in advance

---

This is a sharing dessert, which is not always my favourite way of eating dessert as I'm usually more of an 'all mine' kind of girl, but for this I make an exception. It's a chocolatey set ganache, which sits in a dish, surrounded by home-made pitta chips that are baked in butter, salt and sugar. It's rich and sweet, so I like to drizzle the top with passion fruit pulp to add some freshness.

Start by making the brigadeiro. Add the condensed milk to a non-stick pan along with the cocoa powder and butter and mix everything through.

Have ready a domed bowl, 12–15cm in diameter and large enough to hold all the mixture in the pan. Grease the inside of the bowl and cover the base and inside with clingfilm, making sure to leave some overhanging. Grease inside lightly too.

Pop the condensed milk pan onto a high heat. As soon as it comes to the boil, reduce the heat and mix constantly for 5 minutes until it begins to thicken, then take off the heat. Leave to cool in the pan for

5 minutes before pouring into the prepared bowl. Leave to cool, then chill in the fridge for 4 hours until it's firm to the touch.

Now, get on to the pitta chips. Preheat the oven to 180°C/fan 160°C/gas 4.

Arrange the pitta on a large baking tray lined with baking paper and drizzle with the melted butter, making sure it coats all the pitta chips. Mix the salt and sugar in a bowl and then sprinkle all over the pitta chips. Pop into the oven and bake for 20–25 minutes, turning them halfway so that they get a fair chance of getting crisp on both sides, then take them out and leave to cool on the tray.

When you are ready to serve, pop the bowl of brigadeiro onto a serving dish that's large enough to have the pitta chips around the edge. Dust the pitta chips with cocoa powder, if you like, and lay them all around the bowl. Halve the passion fruits, scoop out the pulp and drizzle all over the brigadeiro.

Take a knife and help yourself to chunks of the brigadeiro, eaten on your crisp salty-sweet pitta chips.

# earl grey sticky toffee pudding

**Serves** 10   **Prep** 40 minutes, plus infusing
and cooling   **Cook** 45 minutes
**Will keep** wrapped and in a tin for 3–4 days
(and sauce will keep in the fridge for 1 week)

**For the cake**

200ml hot water

4 Earl Grey teabags

1 star anise

200g pitted dates

60g unsalted butter,
softened, plus extra for
greasing the tin

200g dark muscovado
sugar

1 teaspoon bicarbonate
of soda

1 medium egg, lightly
beaten

a pinch of salt

200g self-raising flour,
sifted

**For the sauce**

200g dark muscovado
sugar

65g unsalted butter

3 tablespoons treacle

300ml double cream

a pinch of salt

**To serve**

ice cream

This is like any yummy sticky toffee pudding,
but with a slight difference – all the stickiness
of dates and a rich, dark sauce, but enhanced
with the subtle scent of Earl Grey tea.

Start by making the cake. Add the hot water to a jug
along with the teabags and star anise and leave to
infuse for 15 minutes.

Meanwhile, preheat the oven to 180°C/fan 160°C/gas
4 and grease and line the inside of a 900g loaf tin.

Add the pitted dates to a saucepan along with the
butter and sugar. Squeeze the teabags out of the
jug, making sure to really press out all that flavour.
Remove the anise and pour the strained tea into the
pan with the dates.

Put on the stove and bring to the boil, then stir and
take off as soon as the sugar has dissolved and the
butter melted. Leave to cool for 15 minutes. Using a
hand-held blender or food processor blend the
mixture to a smooth paste, then transfer into a bowl.

Add the bicarbonate of soda, egg, salt and flour and
mix by hand, electric whisk or in a free-standing
mixer until you have a smooth batter. Pour it into the
prepared tin and smooth off the edges by tapping on
the worktop. Bake for 40 minutes.

For the sauce, put the sugar, butter and treacle in a
saucepan and place on a medium heat until the
sugar has dissolved and the butter has melted. As
soon as it begins to bubble, take off the heat.

Add the cream and mix in, pop back onto a low heat
and leave to bubble away for 5 minutes until you
have a smooth dark caramel.

Take the cake out of the oven and leave to cool in the
tin for 10 minutes. Remove from the tin onto a serving
dish and cut into 10 slices, angled just slightly, so they
tip a little bit on their sides. Pour the toffee sauce over
generously, making sure to leave some behind for
people who like to pour a little extra, like me!

Serve the pudding while it's still warm, with a mahoosive
dollop of ice cream, and even a hot cup of Earl Grey
alongside!

# jam roly-poly

**For the roly poly**

250g self-raising flour, plus extra for dusting

50g unsalted butter, cold and cubed, plus extra for greasing

1 tablespoon caster sugar

1 teaspoon vanilla bean paste

50g veg suet

150ml cold whole milk (you may need less)

**For the jam filling**

100g fresh raspberries

1 orange, zest only

1 teaspoon caster sugar

**To finish**

50g caster sugar, for dusting

hot custard (see page 118 – Tottenham cake)

fresh mixed berries

---

**Serves** 6　**Prep** 25 minutes
**Cook** 1 hour

---

This is my husband's absolute favourite – he remembers it fondly from his school dinners. Not a memory I share, as we were more cornflake tart and toothpaste tart! Nothing makes me happier than baking this for him (never from frozen – we can't go back to school). My version is made with fresh fruit, a sprinkling of orange zest and a crunchy sugar topping and is served with hot, hot custard and lots of berries.

Start by preheating the oven to 180°C/fan 160°C/gas 4. Place a deep baking tray into the base, add boiling water and close the oven. Make sure there is a rack above the tray, as this is where the jam roly-poly will steam.

Take a 30 x 40cm sheet of foil and a piece of grease-proof paper that is the same size and pop the paper on top of the foil. Grease the paper and set both aside.

Pour the flour into a bowl along with the butter, sugar and vanilla bean paste. Rub the butter in using the tips of your fingers until you have no more massive clumps of butter and the mixture resembles breadcrumbs. You could equally do this using a food processor.

Add the suet and mix in well. Make a well in the centre and add 125ml of the milk to it. Using a cutlery knife, bring the dough together, then get your hands in to bring it into a ball. If the dough is looking dry, add the remaining milk.

Dust the surface with some flour, pop the dough down and roll into a 25cm square.

Crush the raspberries with the orange zest and mix well with the sugar. Spread the fruit onto the dough square, leaving a 1cm edge exposed.

Now roll like you would a Swiss roll, making sure the seam is on the base. Pinch the ends to seal it really well. Pick it up and put into the centre of the paper, seam-side down. Bring the two paper edges to the top and roll to seal, making sure to leave lots of space for the roly-poly to grow. Seal the ends by rolling them up, then put the roly-poly on the rack and steam and bake for 1 hour.

As soon as it is baked, take out and leave to cool for 10 minutes in the paper foil parcel. Unwrap, pop onto a serving dish and sprinkle sugar over generously. Cut into slices while still warm and serve with hot custard and fresh berries.

# filo cream parcels

## For the cream

1.2 litres double cream

120g ground rice or rice flour

100g caster sugar

1 orange, zest only (save the juice for the syrup)

## For the filo casing

270g pack of filo pastry

100g ghee or butter, melted

## For the syrup

200g caster sugar

juice of 1 orange, adding extra water to make up to 200ml

1 teaspoon orange blossom water

3 cardamom pods, seeds removed and crushed

a small pinch of saffron strands

## For decoration

50g pistachios, finely chopped

---

Makes 14   Prep 30 minutes, plus cooling and soaking   Cook 40 minutes
Best eaten on the day they are made but will keep in the fridge for up to 24 hours

---

This is my version of a Lebanese dessert. Filo pastry is filled with a reduced cream thickened with ground rice and then sweetened and flavoured with zingy orange zest. I bake these until they are super crisp to balance out that soft filling. While hot, I drench them in a tangy saffron syrup.

Add the cream to a fairly deep saucepan on a high heat. As soon as it comes to the boil, turn down to a medium heat and keep stirring for about 10 minutes until it has reduced and thickened to make it richer.

Lower the heat, pour in your ground rice and whisk for 2–3 minutes until it really begins to thicken up. As soon as it starts to thicken and come away from the sides, take off the heat, add the sugar and orange zest and mix through. Pour onto a flat plate, smooth out and leave to cool as much as possible.

Preheat the oven to 200°C/fan 180°C/gas 6 and have two large baking trays with sides at the ready.

Cut the pile of rectangular filo sheets down the middle into 14 squares. Lay them out and dollop an equal amount of the cooled cream mixture into the centre of each (if you want to be exact, it's about 85g each).

Take a square, fold one side over, then the next, then the next and then the next, working your way round until you have encased the mound into a neat square, roughly 7cm. Repeat with the remaining squares.

Generously brush the base of the trays with the ghee, add the squares seam-side down and brush the tops with more ghee. Pop into the oven for 15–20 minutes to really crisp up the pastry.

Meanwhile, make the syrup by mixing the sugar, orange juice and water, orange blossom water, cardamom and saffron in a small pan. Give it a stir and, as soon as it comes to the boil, reduce the heat to low and leave for 10 minutes to thicken slightly.

As soon as the pastries are cooked and golden, pop them onto a serving dish and pour the syrup all over to soak into the filo. Leave to soak for 30 minutes.

These can be eaten as they are or are also delicious served chilled, which lets them firm up a little. Sprinkle on a tiny bit of pistachio just before serving.

# sharing chocolate fondant

Serves 4–5    Prep 15 minutes
Cook 22 minutes

100g unsalted butter,
    softened, plus extra for
    greasing the dish

2 tablespoons cocoa
    powder

100g dark chocolate,
    chopped

2 medium eggs

2 medium egg yolks

120g caster sugar

100g plain flour, sifted

**To finish**

crème fraîche to serve

icing sugar for dusting

If you don't mind sharing, this is the one for you. It's like those little melt-in-the-middle chocolate puddings, but a large one. With none of the individual pots, there's less washing up and still all of the deliciousness. But I do often find myself asking, because it is just one pot, does that mean it is technically one portion? Can it all be mine, mine, mine? This is best served hot and enjoyed with a dollop of cooling crème fraîche.

Preheat the oven to 180°C/fan 160°C/gas 4. Start by greasing a 23cm non-stick or enamel pie dish (I use a 22 x 4.5cm deep enamel pie dish). Using a pastry brush, brush the butter on the base and right up the sides of the dish in the same direction until you have covered it all with butter.

Pop into the freezer for 5 minutes. Take out of the freezer, sprinkle over the cocoa powder and tip the dish around so that the butter catches the cocoa. Do this until you have totally covered the dish. Put the dish back into the fridge while you make the batter.

Now, to make the fondant, put the butter into a glass dish along with the chocolate and melt either over a pan of simmering water or in the microwave in 30-second bursts on low, stirring in between. Once the butter and chocolate are totally melted and mixed, leave to cool.

To another bowl add the whole eggs, egg yolks and sugar and whisk till the mixture is light and fluffy. This should take 2–3 minutes using an electric hand whisk on high. Add the melted chocolate and butter mix and whisk in till you have an even mixture. Fold the flour into the wet mixture till there are no more bits of flour.

Take the dish out of the fridge, pour the mixture into the dish and allow it to run and level off naturally. Bake for 17–18 minutes. The fondant should be set around the sides and on top, but still gooey in the middle. As soon as the timer is up, put a plate on top and turn the cake out.

To serve, dust with icing sugar, add a dollop of the crème fraîche and get stuck in while it is still hot. This needs to be eaten straight away as it carries on cooking if left and the gooey middle will start to set – and we don't want that to happen!

# slow-cooker apple and tarragon pudding

**For the apple base**

6 green apples
(you want a sharp
apple, something
with a tang), peeled,
cored and cut into thin
wedges, about 500g
in weight

50g unsalted butter,
melted

25g caster sugar

small handful of fresh
tarragon, leaves
picked and finely
chopped

150g fresh or frozen
blackberries

a pinch of salt

1 x 397g tin of caramel

**For the cakey top**

250g self-raising flour

250g unsalted butter,
softened

250g caster sugar

1 teaspoon vanilla
extract

1 teaspoon almond
extract

**To serve**

hot custard (see page
118 – Tottenham cake)
or ice cream

---

**Serves** 6 **Prep** 25 minutes
**Cook** 5–6 hours in a slow cooker

---

This is the kind of pudding I like to make when my oven is full of everything else and there is no room for pudding – and on no planet is that acceptable. There is always room for pudding, in our hearts, in our kitchens, on our plates! So this is the perfect recipe for such a situation: stewed apples, brought to life with fresh tarragon, topped with a crumb layer that miraculously turns itself into a cakey pudding that's just insanely delicious!

Begin by putting the apple wedges in a slow cooker dish. Add the melted butter and sugar and mix it all through. Now add the chopped tarragon and blackberries and mix through with the pinch of salt.

Level the apple layer off, then spoon in the tin of caramel and create an even layer on top of the apple by spreading it to the edges with the back of a spoon.

To make the cakey top, add the flour and butter to another bowl and rub together until you have a breadcrumby mixture. Add the sugar, vanilla and almond extract and mix until smooth and even – you can do this by hand or in a food processor, whichever you prefer. Spoon the whole lot onto the caramel layer in an even-ish layer.

Pop the dish into the slow cooker, turn onto the lowest setting, put the lid on and leave for 5–6 hours.

Once it's ready, you should be able to spoon the delicious appley, caramelly pudding straight out of the pan. We like to eat this with hot custard and a dollop of ice cream. It's all or nothing here!

# chocolate caramel flan

**Serves** 10–12
**Prep** 40 minutes
**Cook** 1 hour, plus cooling
**Keeps** in the fridge for 2 days

**For the base**

125g salted caramel

**For the cake**

150g unsalted butter, softened, plus extra melted butter for greasing the tin

190g soft brown sugar

1 medium egg

1 tablespoon vanilla bean extract

200g plain flour, sifted, plus extra for flouring the tin

30g cocoa powder

1 teaspoon bicarbonate of soda

1 teaspoon baking powder

3 tablespoons coffee granules

230ml whole milk

**For the crème caramel**

600ml evaporated milk

1 x 397g tin of condensed milk

4 medium eggs

1 teaspoon vanilla bean paste

a pinch of salt

This clever dessert starts with caramel in the base of the tin, then a simple chocolate sponge batter and finally a crème caramel mixture, and as it sits and bakes in a water bath, the crème caramel seeps down to meet the caramel and creates a beautiful soft layer, which becomes the top once the cake is turned out. Just magical!

Preheat the oven to 180°C/fan 160°C/gas 4. Grease and lightly flour the inside of a 23cm bundt tin. Find a roasting tin big enough to hold the bundt tin comfortably and deep enough for water to come two-thirds of the way up the side of the bundt tin. Pop a tea towel into the base of the roasting tin.

Put the salted caramel in a microwaveable dish and warm for just long enough to make it runny, about 20 seconds. Pour into the base of the tin, avoiding drips on the sides. Tap on the worktop to level off.

Make the cake by whisking the butter and sugar in a mixing bowl until you have a really light and fluffy mixture. Add the egg and vanilla extract and mix in.

To a separate bowl, add the flour, cocoa, bicarbonate of soda and baking powder and mix really well.

Now, spoon the coffee into a small bowl, add a few tablespoons of the milk and heat for a few seconds in the microwave until the coffee has dissolved. Mix, pour into the remaining milk and stir through.

Sift a third of the flour mixture onto the butter, sugar and egg mixture and fold in with a large metal spoon. Fold in a third of the milk, then repeat until all the flour and milk has been mixed in.

When you have a smooth batter, spoon over the salted caramel, tap the tin on the worktop to remove any bubbles and make sure you have a level top. Put the bundt tin into the centre of the roasting tin.

Make the crème caramel mixture by mixing the evaporated milk, condensed milk, eggs, vanilla and salt in a food processor until smooth and even. Pour on top of the cake batter and level the top.

Have a jug of hot water ready. Put the roasting tin with the bundt tin into the oven. Before you close the door, pour the water straight onto the tea towel in the roasting tin, making sure the water reaches at least two-thirds of the way up. Bake for 1 hour and don't be tempted to open the oven. Once cooked, take out and leave to cool in the tin for another hour, then flip over onto a serving dish and it is ready to eat.

desserts                                                                    115

# croissant
# ice cream
# pudding

butter, at room
    temperature, for
    greasing the dish
    and spreading

4 large croissants

170g marmalade, fine
    shred or smooth,
    whatever you prefer

350g vanilla ice cream,
    softened

60g dark chocolate,
    chopped

icing sugar, for dusting

**Serves** 6    **Prep** 10 minutes, plus 10 minutes
standing    **Cook** 10–12 minutes

This is based on a bread-and-butter pudding, but made with croissants because they are much more buttery, then smothered with extra butter and lashings of thick marmalade. It's also much faster than a regular bread-and-butter pudding because I'm making it with ice cream – not just popping some on the side or on top, but actually making the pudding with it! Traditionally made with custard and milk, it seemed like the perfect short cut. Sprinkle with some dark chocolate and this might be the fastest and most buttery pudding you will make, ever.

Preheat the oven to 200°C/fan 180°C/gas 6. Start by greasing a medium rectangular roasting dish with some butter, be generous!

Slice the croissants lengthways, all the way. Butter the inside of all eight slices with a thin layer of butter, then take the marmalade and spread with a layer of that.

Place the croissants into the dish, laying them in some sort of neat fashion. Take dollops of the ice cream, dot around sporadically and leave to just melt a little for 10 minutes. It won't melt completely, the structure will still be quite fluffy on top.

Sprinkle the chocolate over. Pop into the oven and bake for 10–12 minutes. Dust with some icing sugar and it is ready to eat.

# chai chia puddings

60g chia seeds

400ml hazelnut milk

3 tablespoons chai spice mix (see page 164)

2 tablespoons maple syrup, plus extra for drizzling

1 mango, diced, about 325g

200g mango pulp (if you can't find any you can make this by just whizzing up some chopped mango)

200g Greek yoghurt

40g roasted chopped hazelnuts

Chia seeds are not just for breakfast, they are for pudding too. When you leave them to soak in nut milk they make a thick, creamy pudding, my version of which is fragrantly delicious with chai spices, served with chopped mango and topped with yoghurt, maple syrup and roasted hazelnuts. I think I just like saying chai chia. Go on, say it. It rolls off the tongue!

This is super simple. Pop the chia seeds into a bowl along with the hazelnut milk and mix really well. Sprinkle in the chai spices and the maple syrup and mix again well.

Cover with some clingfilm and leave for at least 4 hours to allow the chia seeds to bloom (there's nothing worse than crunchy, unbloomed chia seeds). Alternatively, use a plastic container with a lid rather than a bowl and clingfilm.

The next stage is to add the chopped mango and stir through. This is perfect to leave overnight if you are doing it for breakfast, but do this at breakfast time if you are making the puddings for lunch or dinner.

Take four empty jam jars or glass serving dishes. Equally divide the mango pulp among the jars, then the chia pudding. Add the yoghurt and drizzle over some maple syrup. Sprinkle the hazelnuts over and these are ready to serve.

# tottenham cake
## with custard

**Makes** 24 small squares and 1 litre of custard
**Prep** 35 minutes   **Cook** 45 minutes, plus
cooling   **Will keep** in a tin for up to 3 days
(and custard will keep in fridge for up to 3 days)

This cake was first invented in 1901, in Tottenham no less. A sponge cake topped with a pink icing that was originally coloured using mulberries, I would like to say that my first experience of this steeped-in-history baked treat was driven by my need for baking knowledge, but sadly not. This was the cake I remembered from school lunchtimes: simple, delicious and sweet, all doused in hot custard. I had forgotten about it until I recently stopped off at a high-street bakery and there it was again, though with less appeal when there is no queue to wait in or teenagers to fend off. My purchase didn't match up to my memories, so I decided to try making it for myself, and here's the outcome. Don't get me wrong though, on a busy day I would very happily devour the bakery-bought variety.

## For the cake

225g unsalted butter, softened, plus extra for greasing the tin

225g caster sugar

4 medium eggs

1 teaspoon vanilla bean extract

1 teaspoon almond extract

300g self-raising flour, sifted

1 teaspoon baking powder

4 tablespoons whole milk

## For the icing

100g fresh raspberries

350g icing sugar, sifted

## For the custard

200ml double cream

700ml whole milk

4 egg yolks

3 tablespoons cornflour

100g caster sugar

1 teaspoon vanilla bean extract

2 teaspoons almond extract

Start by making the cake. Preheat the oven to 180°C/ fan 160°C/gas 4 and line and grease a 30 x 20cm rectangle traybake tin.

Add the butter to a bowl with the sugar and beat until the mixture is light and fluffy and almost white. Now add the eggs, one at a time, until incorporated. Add the vanilla, almond extract, flour, baking powder and milk and fold through until all the flour has disappeared. Pour into the prepared tin and level off, then bake for 30–35 minutes, until a skewer inserted comes out clean. Take out and leave to cool completely in the tin.

Make the icing by crushing the raspberries using the back of a fork until you have no lumps, apart from the seeds of course. Add the icing sugar and mix until you have a beautiful pink icing, with not just colour, but also that fresh raspberry flavour.

Tip the cake out onto a serving dish and then smother all over with the pink icing.

Let's get on to that custard by adding the cream and milk to a pan, gently bringing the mixture to a boil and then turning the heat off.

Add the egg yolks, cornflour, sugar, vanilla and almond extract to a bowl and whisk to a smooth paste. Now, in a gentle stream, add the hot milk mixture, a little at a time, whisking all the time. Once all the milk has been added, pour back into the pan, pop back onto a low to medium heat and stir until the custard coats the back of the spoon. Take off the heat and transfer to a pouring jug.

Now you are ready to eat your soft cake, with its sweet icing, all doused in hot custard. Just like in high school.

# chapter five

# CELEBRATION BAKES

# mango and coconut yoghurt cake with german buttercream

**For the cake**

butter, for greasing the tins

50g desiccated coconut

1 mango, peeled and thinly sliced lengthways

400g Greek yoghurt

300g caster sugar

7 medium eggs, lightly beaten

400g self-raising flour

1 teaspoon baking powder

a pinch of salt

**For the German buttercream**

150ml whole milk

100g caster sugar

3 egg yolks

1 tablespoon cornflour

350g unsalted butter, at room temperature

½ teaspoon vanilla extract

**For the decoration**

25g coconut chips or desiccated coconut, toasted

150g mango pulp

**To serve**

Greek yoghurt and extra mango pulp

**Serves** 8–10  **Prep** 35 minutes, plus chilling  **Cook** 45 minutes

These flavours are as traditional as they get for me. They're the flavours I grew up with, though while mango was cooked in curries, dried or eaten in the sun under the shade of the tree, it was never put in a cake! The same went for coconut. If it wasn't being eaten dry, it was being stewed or eaten early, drinking its sweet water and scooping out its young flesh, but never ever in a cake. So, let's fix that, and put all that wonderful stuff straight into a cake, shall we?

Preheat the oven to 180°C/fan 160°C/gas 4. Line the bases and grease two 20cm deep round cake tins.

Toast the coconut in a small pan until it is golden and sprinkle into the bases of the cake tins, making sure to evenly distribute it. Toasting it will enhance the flavour (untoasted coconut is no different to the wood chip shavings I lay out for my rabbit). Add the mango in some sort of orderly fashion, straight on top of that coconut.

The cake is an all-in-one method, so really easy. Pop the yoghurt into a large mixing bowl along with the sugar, eggs, flour, baking powder and salt and

→

mix until you have a smooth, shiny cake batter. Pour the mixture into the tins and tap the tins a few times on the work surface to level off the top. Bake for 40–45 minutes until golden and a skewer inserted comes out clean. Take the cakes out and leave in the tins to cool for 15 minutes, then turn out and leave to cool completely.

Meanwhile, make the buttercream by adding the milk to a saucepan with the sugar. As soon as it just comes to the boil, take off the heat and mix, making sure the sugar has melted.

Now add the egg yolks to a bowl with the cornflour and whisk. In a steady stream pour in the hot milk mixture, making sure to stir all of the time. Pour the mixture back into the pan and heat gently until it all thickens into a really thick custard that coats the back of the spoon. Transfer to a large bowl, cover with clingfilm and leave to cool, then chill in the fridge.

When chilled, whisk the custard mix, then add a good tablespoon of butter at a time, whisking after each addition. Keep whisking until you have a really stiff, pipeable buttercream. Pop into a piping bag.

Take the first cake, with the fruit side facing upwards, and arrange on a serving dish. Pipe swirls of the buttercream all around the edge and then in the centre, covering the top of the cake. Pop the other cake on top and make the same swirls around the edge, avoiding the middle and leaving gaps between the swirls.

Pour the mango pulp into the centre, allowing it to drip down the sides. Sprinkle it with the toasted coconut and serve the cake with Greek yoghurt.

# honey cake with salted hazelnuts

Serves 10    Prep 1 hour, plus chilling
Cook 26–28 minutes (baking in four batches of two biscuits)

**For the cake**

80g unsalted butter

270g runny honey

120g golden caster sugar

2 medium eggs, lightly beaten

1 teaspoon bicarbonate of soda

500g plain flour, sifted, plus extra for dusting

**For the filling**

600ml soured cream

80g icing sugar

250ml double cream

65g runny honey

1 teaspoon vanilla bean paste

**For the decoration**

100g roasted chopped hazelnuts

½ teaspoon salt

fresh berries

This looks like a cake, but in fact it's made with eight biscuit-like rounds that are flavoured with honey and browned butter, then moistened with a sweet and slightly sour cream and stacked up. The end result is round and cuts like a cake, so that's what I'm calling it, but to be honest I don't care about labels, all I know is it's delicious.

Put the butter in a small saucepan, bring to the boil, then reduce the heat and let it begin to brown. As soon as the little grains of milk solids become dark, take off the heat. Add the honey and sugar and heat until the sugar has dissolved, then tip into a large bowl and leave to cool for 15 minutes.

Add the eggs and mix well. Now add the bicarbonate of soda and the flour and mix till a smooth dough forms. Cover and chill in the fridge for at least 2 hours.

Roll the dough into a sausage shape and divide into eight equal pieces. You can weigh them if you want to be exact. Dust the work surface and your hands generously and shape the eight pieces into balls.

Line two baking trays with baking paper and preheat the oven to 180°C/fan 160°C/gas 4. Find an 18cm round template (e.g. a plate or the base of a cake tin).

Dust a ball of dough with flour, then place between two sheets of baking paper and roll out to about 3mm thick. Use the template to cut it into a circle, being sure to keep all of the scraps. Repeat with all eight balls.

Pop the circles onto the baking trays (however many will fit) and bake for just 5 minutes. As soon as they are baked, take off the tray, pop onto a wire rack and repeat until you have done all eight.

Arrange the scraps in an even layer across the two trays and bake for about 6–8 minutes until they are really crisp and golden. Take them out and leave to one side.

Make the filling by mixing together the soured cream and the icing sugar really well. Add the double cream to a bowl and whip to soft peaks. Fold in the soured cream mixture, honey and vanilla.

It is best to assemble this cake directly onto your serving plate (one that can fit in your fridge). Use a dab of the cream to secure the first circle onto the serving dish. Drop about 5 tablespoons of the cream mixture on top and carefully spread evenly all over. Put the next circle on and repeat until you have done all eight layers.

You should have enough cream to cover the top and sides, so do exactly that and smooth over as best you can. It doesn't have to be perfect, because we are going to really cover this up.

Put the baked scraps in a food processor and blitz to a fine crumb. Mix in the roasted hazelnuts and salt.

For extra decoration I like to use a template to create a heart shape in the crumbs on the top of the cake, but choose whatever shape you like — even use a doily, if you can find one or know what one is! If you don't want to use a template, just mark a heart (or other shape) on the icing with a table knife and use that as a guide for where to stick the crumbs.

Take the crumbs and gently press them onto the sides and the top around your template, if using, before removing it. You might have to pipe more icing onto your shape to neaten up the edges. Now put into the fridge to set and chill.

Serve with some fresh berries.

# berry hot cross buns

**For the dough**

300ml whole milk

50g unsalted butter

500g strong bread flour, plus extra for dusting

75g caster sugar

1 teaspoon salt

7g fast-action yeast

1 medium egg, lightly beaten

oil, for greasing the bowl

75g dried cranberries, roughly chopped

50g dried blueberries, roughly chopped

1 orange, zest only

**For the berry cross**

9g tube of freeze-dried strawberries or raspberries

75g plain flour, sifted

90ml water

**For the filling and glaze**

300g jar of seedless berry jam (strawberry, raspberry, whatever you fancy)

3 tablespoons golden syrup

---

**Makes** 15    **Prep** 40 minutes, plus rising
**Cook** 20 minutes    **Best eaten** on day they are made

---

I have to admit that hot cross buns were one of my least favourite things growing up. Not that my parents bought them often, but at Easter time we'd have them at school and I never liked the flavour. It's still not my favourite, but the less my body needs butter, the more I crave it. These are a step up from regular hot cross buns, the dough crammed with all the fruitiness of berries, and there's no reason to cut and toast them because they are already filled to the seam with jam. The finishing touch is a pink cross to match!

Start by making the dough. Add the milk to a saucepan with the butter, heat until the butter has melted and take off the heat.

→

Add the flour to a large bowl and mix in the sugar. Add the salt on one side of the flour and the yeast to the other side.

Make a well in the centre, drop in the egg and then add the warm milk mixture and roughly mix using the back of a spoon or palette knife, then get your hands in and bring the dough together.

On a lightly floured surface, knead the dough until it is smooth and stretchy. This will take about 10 minutes and lots of elbow grease. Or you can do it in a free-standing mixer with a dough hook attached, which should take about 6 minutes on a medium speed. Pop the dough into a greased bowl and leave to double in size in a warm place.

Line a large baking tray or two smaller trays with some baking paper. Tip the dough out onto a lightly floured surface and knock all of that air out. Spread the dough out into a circle and sprinkle on the cranberries, blueberries and orange zest, then knead the lot in until the fruit is evenly distributed.

Take the dough and divide into 15 portions. Roll each dough ball until it has a smooth surface and pop onto the tray or trays with about a 3cm gap between each one to give them space to prove and grow. Leave in a warm spot, covered in some greased clingfilm, to double in size.

Preheat the oven to 200°C/fan 180°C/gas 6.

Now to make the flour paste for the cross. Pound the strawberries or raspberries in a pestle and mortar or blitz in a food processor until you have a fine pink dust. Add this to a bowl with the flour and water and mix to a smooth, pipeable paste. Spoon into a piping bag. Uncover the proven dough and pipe a thin cross on each bun.

Bake the buns for 18–20 minutes. As soon as they are golden brown and bounce back when touched, take them out of the oven and leave to cool on a cooling rack. Then use the handle of a teaspoon or the end of a dinner knife to make a hole in the side of each bun without going all the way through. You are creating a cavity to fill with delicious jam.

Pop the jam into a piping bag and pipe it into the hole of each hot cross bun, until full. You will know when it is as the piping bag will naturally force itself out. Put the buns back onto the tray. Warm the golden syrup just to make it runny and brush all over the buns to give them that sweet, sticky glaze. Filled, fruity and ready to eat!

celebration cakes

# zesty fruitcake

**For the cake**

1 grapefruit, ½ the juice and zest

1 orange, juice and zest

1 lemon, juice and zest

1 lime, juice and zest

250g dates, pitted and chopped

100g mixed peel

100g glacé cherries, chopped

400g currants

1 large very ripe banana, mashed

4 medium eggs

225g unsalted butter, softened, plus extra for greasing the tin

2 tablespoons whole milk

300g plain flour, sifted

2 teaspoons mixed spice

1 teaspoon baking powder

**For the decoration**

4 tablespoons apricot jam

500g yellow marzipan

icing sugar, for dusting

500g white fondant

> **Serves** 12–14    **Prep** 50 minutes
> **Cook** 1¾ hours

Fruitcake takes me back to being in high school, where they made a tame version with just a smattering of fruit for our south Asian palates, which perhaps they thought couldn't cope with all the flavours of the 'West'. It was delicious, but I couldn't understand why there was not as much fruit in it as the ones I remembered seeing on the telly. I love fruitcake just as it is, slabs cut out, with cheese, or custard. This is my very zesty version, sharp from all the citrus, sweet from the dried fruit and dates, but free from refined sugar. It simply doesn't need it. It's delicious enough as it is. But you can, if you want, add a layer of marzipan and fondant, especially if it's for a special occasion or Christmas. Or even if it's just for you – because fruitcake is not just for Christmas and weddings!

Preheat the oven to 160°C/fan 140°C/gas 3. Grease and line the base and sides of a 23cm round spring-form tin with baking paper. Grease again and line a second time, make sure to trim off any excess paper at the top so the paper is in line flush with the top of the tin.

Put the zest of the grapefruit, orange, lemon and lime into a large bowl. Squeeze all the citrus fruit juice into a jug. We need 200ml of liquid, so if the juice squeezed doesn't come up to 200ml, top up with orange juice.

Now add the dates, mixed peel, cherries and currants to the bowl with the zest. Add the juice and mix through, then leave the fruit to absorb all the moisture. Add the mashed banana and mix.

In a separate bowl, whisk the eggs and butter until well combined. Add the milk, flour, mixed spice and baking powder and mix to an evenly distributed batter. It might look a little curdled, but this doesn't matter, it bakes just fine.

Add the fruit mixture and mix through until all the fruit is covered in the batter. Spoon the mixture into the prepared tin and level off the top. Take a large piece of foil, cover the top and secure the foil around the edge. Bake on the middle shelf for 1 hour.

After an hour, take the cake out, remove the foil and bake for another 30–45 minutes until golden and firm on top and a skewer inserted in the middle comes out with no raw batter attached. Take the cake out of the oven, place onto a cooling rack and leave the cake in the tin for 30 minutes, before turning out onto the cooling rack and leaving to cool completely.

If you are decorating the cake, once it has cooled completely, melt the jam in a small pan until it is liquid enough to brush on. Brush the surface.

Roll out the marzipan on a surface lightly dusted with icing sugar to a 5mm thickness and large enough to cover the top. Use the cake tin as a template to cut a perfect circle. Take the marzipan circle and place on top of the cake onto the apricot jam and smooth over using the palm of your hand.

Brush again with the leftover jam. Roll the fondant out in the same way as the marzipan and cut a circle out. Pop on top of the marzipan and press gently so it adheres to the marzipan layer.

Use any leftover marzipan and fondant to decorate the top. I quite like to keep it simple and to just use the back of a cutlery knife to scallop the edges.

# pull-apart muffin cake

**For the Swiss meringue buttercream**

245g egg whites

345g caster sugar

600g unsalted butter, softened

**For the chocolate salted caramel**

175g soft brown sugar

50g unsalted butter, softened

½ teaspoon salt

150ml double cream

200g dark chocolate, chopped or chips

**For the cupcakes**

250g unsalted butter, softened

250g caster sugar

4 medium eggs, lightly beaten

a pinch of salt

250g self-raising flour, sifted

6 tablespoons cocoa powder

75ml whole milk

**For the decoration**

15 marshmallows (regular sized)

glacé cherries

rainbow sprinkles

**Makes** 24 cakes  **Prep** 1½ hours
**Cook** 40 minutes

This cake can be as large or as small as you want. What I love about it is that there is no cutting or slicing or plating involved, as it's made from cupcakes, which are filled with a chocolate salted caramel, then wedged together and iced with a delicious Swiss meringue buttercream, all to look like one single cake!

Begin by making the Swiss meringue buttercream. Put the egg whites and sugar in a large bowl and mix together. It will feel stiff, but try to incorporate them.

Find a pan that the bowl will sit on comfortably. Add about 4cm of water to the base of the pan and bring to the boil, then lower the heat to medium and pop a tea towel on top, so it is just covering the pan but

not touching the water. This is going to act like a hammock for the bowl, so set your bowl straight on top and mix constantly for about 15–20 minutes. The aim is for the mixture to get to about 72 degrees and the sugar to dissolve – you will need a thermometer for this.

As soon as it reaches the right temperature, take off the heat and transfer the mixture to the bowl of a free-standing mixer. Whisk on high for about 10–15 minutes until the bowl becomes cool to the touch and the meringue is stiff.

Now take off the whisk attachment and replace it with the paddle attachment. Pinch off 5cm-sized pieces of butter and drop them into the mixture, waiting for each one to be incorporated before

→

adding the next. Continue until you have used up all the butter. The mixture will appear liquid, but keep mixing for another 5–10 minutes and it will thicken and come together. As soon as it's no longer runny and you can spoon it up, it is ready. If you find the mixture is still runny, pop the bowl in the fridge to cool for 2 hours, then start mixing it again. It should then really thicken up enough to be able to pipe beautifully. Set the buttercream to one side or pop it in the fridge if you are using it later.

Make the caramel by adding the sugar and butter to a pan and heating until the sugar dissolves. As soon as it begins to boil, take off the heat, mix in the salt and cream, then pop it back onto the hob and heat for another 3 minutes until it begins to bubble and

thicken. Have the chocolate ready in a bowl. Pour the hot caramel all over it and mix until the chocolate has melted. Leave to cool to the side.

Now let's get on to making the cupcakes. Line two 12-hole muffin tins with cupcake cases. Preheat the oven to 190°C/fan 170°C/gas 5 and make sure you have two shelves free for your trays.

Add the butter and sugar to a mixing bowl and beat until the mixture is light and fluffy. Add the eggs one at a time with the salt, and then add the flour and cocoa powder and fold through until you have a smooth batter. Finally, fold in the milk to loosen the batter a little.

Dollop into the cupcake cases and tap the tins sharply on the work surface to level off. Bake for 15 minutes.

Take out of the oven and leave in the tins for 10 minutes, then lift out of the tins and leave to cool on a wire rack. As soon as the muffins are totally cool, which won't take long, use an apple corer to remove the centre of each cake, making sure not to go all the way to the base.

Pop the caramel into a piping bag and fill each cavity. Using the little rounded tops of the cakes you just pulled out, cover the tops – the rest of it you can nibble on.

Now get yourself a big rectangular serving board. Remove the cupcakes from their paper cases and place them in a rectangle shape, four cupcakes by six, to make 24. Once you know exactly where they

are going, get some of that meringue buttercream and dollop a little on each base to just secure them in place and stop them moving around.

Fill each diamond-shaped gap between the muffins with a marshmallow. Now we are ready to ice. Dollop equal amounts of buttercream on top of each muffin and, using a spatula, spread as if you were icing just one cake, ice the sides then neaten up the edges and level off the top. It should look like one large rectangular cake. Pop the remaining buttercream into a piping bag and pipe kisses all around the edge. Pop a little cherry on top of each, a scattering of rainbow sprinkles and all it needs is candles and 24 people!

# cola cake

**Serves** 9–12
**Prep** 40 minutes
**Cook** 55 minutes
**Keeps** in the fridge for 2 days

**For the cake**

unsalted butter, for greasing the tin

225g plain flour, sifted

225g caster sugar

85g cocoa powder, sieved

1½ teaspoons baking powder

1½ teaspoons bicarbonate of soda

2 teaspoons espresso powder

250ml whole milk

2 medium eggs

125ml oil

250ml cola, reserving the extra 80ml from the can

**For the caramel**

330ml can of cola, plus the extra 80ml

1 tablespoon dark brown sugar

juice of ½ lime (1 tablespoon)

30g unsalted butter

150ml double cream

a pinch of ground cinnamon

**For the buttercream**

100g vegetable fat, at room temperature

100g full-fat cream cheese

400g icing sugar, sieved

1 teaspoon vanilla bean extract

I'm not a massive fan of cola as a drink, because although I quite like the flavour, my body just doesn't appreciate the carbonated element. There's nothing worse than needing to burp when I'm midway through a meeting, or talking to other parents at the school gate, or just trying to do life. So I have found a different use for cola and added it to a cake instead!

Preheat the oven to 180°C/fan 160°C/gas 4. Line and grease a 24cm square cake tin.

Add the flour, sugar, cocoa powder, baking powder, bicarbonate of soda and espresso powder to a large bowl and mix until fully combined.

Add the milk, eggs and oil to a jug and whisk well. Pour into the dry mixture and mix. Now add your cola, whisk until you have a very liquid batter and pour into the prepared tin. Bake on the middle shelf for 55 minutes.

Meanwhile, make the caramel by adding the cola to a small saucepan and bringing to the boil. As soon as it's boiling, reduce the heat just very slightly and allow it to boil for 18–20 minutes, until the mixture is syrupy and really reduced.

Take off the heat and add the sugar, lime juice and butter and mix through until the butter has melted. Add the cream and cinnamon and mix. Don't worry if the cream thickens up, it will become liquid again when it is heated. Return to a low to medium heat and simmer for 5–10 minutes, stirring constantly until you have a delicious dark caramel. Set aside.

As soon as the cake is done, leave in the tin for 10 minutes before cooling on a cooling rack.

Make the buttercream by adding the vegetable fat and cream cheese to a bowl. Whisk together then add the icing sugar a few spoons at a time, incorporating slowly to allow the sugar to melt or you will get a grainy buttercream. Mix in the vanilla.

Pop the icing into a piping bag and pipe in waves or peaks, lines or swirls as you prefer. Drizzle your cooled caramel all over the top, being very generous, and your cake is ready to go.

# pear and ricotta marble cake

Serves 12  Prep 25 minutes
Cook 40 minutes

This light Italian cake is traditionally made with yoghurt, but I make mine with ricotta, which makes it just a little bit (and I mean fractionally) richer. This version is marbled with lemon and chocolate, and each serving has a quarter of a cooked pear to top it off.

Start by quickly but gently cooking the pears (you can use tinned pears instead if you want to save time). Pop the pear quarters into a microwaveable dish, add a splash of water, cover with clingfilm and cook on high for 4 minutes. As soon as they are done and just soft, drain on some kitchen paper and set aside.

Preheat the oven to 180°C/fan 160°C/gas 4 and generously grease a ring cake tin or a shallower bundt tin – a 24cm or 28cm ring mould would be perfect.

**For the cake**

3 pears, peeled, cored and quartered (leaving the stalks on)

butter or oil, for greasing the tin

200g ricotta

300g caster sugar

4 medium eggs, separated

300g plain flour, sifted

10g cornflour

90ml whole milk

1 teaspoon baking powder

1 teaspoon almond extract

1 lemon, zest only

cocoa powder

2 tablespoons cocoa powder, for dusting

Mix the ricotta and sugar together really well. Add the egg yolks, flour, cornflour, milk, baking powder and almond extract and mix through to create a smooth cake batter.

Whisk the egg whites to stiff peaks and gently fold the whites a third at a time into the cake batter until you have a much lighter cake batter.

Separate one half of the batter into another bowl. Add the lemon zest to one and the cocoa powder to the other and gently fold through.

Add the batter to the tin, alternating between the cocoa and lemon until you have finished all the batter, then swirl it all through using a skewer. Put the pear quarters into the tin, stalk side up and leaning on to the edge.

Bake for 35 minutes. Leave in the tin for 10 minutes, then gently take out. Once cooled, dust with some cocoa powder and you are ready to eat.

# praline king cake

**Serves** 10 **Prep** 50 minutes, plus rising **Cook** 40 minutes

## For the 'cake'

600g strong bread flour, plus extra for dusting

100g unsalted butter, melted and cooled

7g fast-action yeast

7g salt

40g caster sugar

230ml whole milk

2 medium eggs

butter, cooking oil

spray or cake release, for greasing the tin

## For the praline filling

70g caster sugar

40g pecans

225g full-fat cream cheese

1 teaspoon vanilla extract

1 teaspoon almond extract

## For the icing

200g icing sugar, sieved

2–3 tablespoons cold water

## To finish

50g desiccated coconut

green gel food colouring

yellow gel food colouring

The clue is in the name here. This is quite some cake, though technically it's more like a sweet bread. It is filled with praline cream and decorated with icing and coloured sugar, typically green and yellow. I'm using coloured desiccated coconut instead, but you can stick to sugar if you like your cake super sweet. I've tried the real thing in New Orleans and it's delicious!

Start by making the dough. Add the flour to a mixing bowl with the butter, yeast, salt and sugar and mix until combined. Make a well in the centre. Measure out the milk into a jug, add the eggs and whisk just to break up the eggs. If the liquid in the jug does not come up to 350ml, add more milk until it does.

Pour in and mix until the dough comes together. Using a free-standing mixer with a dough hook, knead for 5 minutes on medium until the dough is stretchy and elastic. Cover with some clingfilm and leave for about 2 hours to double in size.

To make the praline, line a small tray with some baking paper. Add the sugar to a small pan in an even layer, breaking up any clumps before heating it. Pop onto a medium heat and you will see it caramelizing and melting around the edges. As soon as it does, begin mixing and as soon as the sugar has dissolved and is a golden amber, take off the heat. Add the pecans, stir fast and pour out onto the baking paper, making sure to flatten out. Leave to set completely. As soon as it has, blitz to rough crumbs in a food processor.

When you are ready to shape the dough, add the cream cheese to a bowl with the vanilla, almond extract and praline crumble mix and stir really well.

Tip the dough out onto a lightly floured surface and roll out to a 40cm square. Take a 2-litre bundt tin, the least intricate that you can find, and grease generously with butter, cooking oil spray or cake release.

Tip the cream mixture into the centre of the dough square and spread an even layer all over, leaving just a 1cm edge. Roll up like a Swiss roll. Now gently pick up and pop in the tin, making sure the seam is touching the small inner ring. Pinch the ends together. Cover and leave to prove until doubled in size.

When the dough has nearly doubled, preheat the oven to 200°C/fan 180°C/gas 6. Bake for 35–40 minutes.

Meanwhile, make the icing by mixing the icing sugar and water until you have a thick icing.

Take the cake out and leave to cool on a cooling rack. As soon as it is totally cool, pop a tray underneath to catch spillage and drizzle the icing all over the top, allowing it to run freely down the sides.

Divide the desiccated coconut between two sandwich bags. Pop some different coloured food colouring into each one and, using your fingers, massage the colouring in. If you want to avoid using plastic bags, use bowls, using the back of a dessert spoon to work the colour into the coconut. Alternating the colours, sprinkle the coconut onto the iced cake.

# kouign amann
## sugar crunch pastry square

Serves 6    Prep 30 minutes, plus rising and chilling    Cook 45 minutes

300g strong white flour, plus extra for dusting

5g fast-action yeast

1 teaspoon salt

200ml warm water

25g unsalted butter, melted, plus extra for greasing the tray

250g unsalted butter, in a block

125g demerara sugar, plus extra for sprinkling

1 teaspoon vanilla powder or vanilla bean paste

butter, for greasing the tray

Kouign amann are delicious yeasted, layered, buttery, sugar-filled parcels from Brittany in France. They are to die for! The first time I had them was about 4 years ago when my friend Jonny made them, in his lounge pants, whilst also baking cookies with my kids. I wish he could make them every other weekend for me, but seeing as he has a life and stuff to do, I had to learn to make them myself! In this recipe I've adapted them into one large parcel to cut and share.

To begin, put the flour into the bowl of a free-standing mixer fitted with a dough hook. Add the yeast to one side of the bowl and the salt to the other.

Now, add the water and melted butter and mix on a slow speed until it comes together, then turn the mixer up and knead for 6 minutes. If you are doing it by hand, flour the surface lightly and knead until you have a dough that is smooth, stretchy and elastic. Cover with clingfilm and leave until doubled in size.

Sandwich the block of butter between two sheets of clingfilm and roll out with a rolling pin to a 14cm square. Pop into the fridge and leave to chill.

Take the dough out and, on a floured surface, roll out to a 20cm square. Place the butter in the centre of the dough diagonally, so that each side of the butter faces a corner of the dough. Fold the corners of the dough over the butter to enclose it like an envelope. You should have what looks like an x in the middle made by the joining seams.

Roll the dough into a 45 x 15cm rectangle. Fold the bottom third of dough up over the middle third, then fold the top third of the dough over. If you look from the side, you will now have a sandwich of three layers of butter and three layers of dough. Wrap in clingfilm and place in the fridge for 30 minutes.

Repeat this process twice more, making sure to chill the dough for 30 minutes between folding. Roll the dough into a rectangle, sprinkle with the sugar and fold into thirds again. Working quickly, roll the dough into a large, 30cm square. Mix the sugar with the vanilla powder or paste. Sprinkle the dough with the sugar mixture.

Lightly grease a large baking tray and put the square of pastry straight on.

Take each corner of the pastry and bring into the centre of the square, pushing the pastry into the

centre to keep the dough in place – you should have a beautiful flower shape. Sprinkle with more sugar and leave to puff up, covered with a sheet of greased clingfilm, for just 15 minutes.

Preheat the oven to 220°C/fan 200°C/gas 7. Remove the clingfilm and bake for 40–45 minutes, covering with foil halfway through if it begins to brown too much. Remove from the oven and leave to cool for a couple of minutes before lifting onto a cooling rack.

I love to eat this warm, though it is just as delicious a few hours later. My Achilles heel, I love this sweet crisp goodness with a cup of tea, on the floor in front of the gas fire, just like I did all those years ago with Jonny and the kids!

# cranberry and chilli brioche wreath

| | |
|---|---|
| **Serves** 8 **Prep** 40 minutes, plus overnight proving **Cook** 20 minutes | |

4 large eggs

20ml whole milk

350g strong bread flour, plus extra for dusting

7g fast-action yeast

30g caster sugar

5g salt

2 teaspoons chilli flakes

200g dried cranberries, chopped

200g unsalted butter, softened and cubed

1 x 250g Camembert with a wooden casing

**To finish**

1 egg, lightly beaten

a good pinch of sea salt

2 tablespoons fine-shred marmalade

Any recipe where there is bread and cheese involved, I am there! Every time my tummy rumbles, I hear it say 'bread and cheese, please'. I don't ask for much, so usually it's just a very thick slice of brown bread all smothered in butter, too cold out of the fridge, covered by an unevenly sliced slab of cheese. But occasionally I like to fancy things up and, my goodness, is this recipe worth the time! A beautiful wreath of chilli-laced brioche balls surround a baked Camembert that's topped with a dollop of marmalade. Expect a flavour explosion of sweet and savoury, all soft and oozy, and impossible not to love.

Whisk the eggs and milk to incorporate.

Add the flour, yeast, sugar and salt to another bowl and mix until well combined. Add the chilli flakes and the cranberries and mix through. Make a well in the centre, add the milk mixture and bring the dough roughly together. The mixture will look quite wet and more like a very thick cake batter, but don't worry. Using a free-standing mixer with a dough hook attached, slowly add the butter a little at a time until you have used it all up, then knead the dough on a fast setting for 10 minutes. Cover, pop into the fridge and leave to prove overnight.

Next day, line a large baking tray with some baking paper. Take the bottom half of the wooden casing the cheese comes in and put it in the centre of the baking tray. Put the cheese back in the fridge.

Tip the dough out onto a lightly floured surface and knock the air back. Roll out into a sausage shape and divide into 5 equal pieces. Divide each one into 5, so you have 25 little dough balls. Pinch each ball into the centre, turn seam-side down and roll around in your hand to create a smooth ball. Arrange the first 10 around the wooden cheese case and then the following 15 around them, leaving small gaps to allow them to prove. Cover with some greased clingfilm and leave until doubled in size.

Preheat the oven to 190°C/fan 170°C/gas 5. Take the cheese out of the wrapper and pop into the wooden casing. Brush the dough balls with the beaten egg and sprinkle all over with a generous helping of salt. Bake for 20 minutes.

Add spoonfuls of marmalade to the hot cheese and you are ready to eat.

→

celebration cakes

# middle of the table nut roast

**Serves** 8–10
**Prep** 30 minutes, plus cooling **Cook** 1½ hours

20g unsalted butter, plus extra for greasing the tin

4 cloves of garlic, finely grated

1 red onion, finely diced

2 tablespoons tomato purée

200g chestnut mushrooms, finely chopped

1 large carrot, grated (about 150g)

1 teaspoon salt

1 teaspoon chilli powder

1 teaspoon ground cumin

½ teaspoon ground turmeric

150g red split lentils

400ml vegetable stock

100g fine dried breadcrumbs

150g mixed nuts, finely chopped

3 medium eggs, lightly beaten

100g mature Cheddar cheese, finely grated

a small handful of fresh coriander, finely chopped

**For the flavour glaze**

1 tablespoon yeast extract

1 tablespoon hot water

1 tablespoon ketchup

For a long time I had a preconceived notion that a nut roast couldn't be yummy, because it was a replacement for meat, but recently I realized how wrong I was. A nut roast shouldn't be seen as a substitute or replacement, but as the centrepiece to your meal, sitting proud, pretty and delicious for everyone to enjoy! This is the kind of thing that if not finished can be eaten cold and sliced the next day, with a salad or – the way I like to eat it – sandwiched between a heavily buttered, overly floured bap, the size of my head, with the biggest squirt of brown sauce!

Preheat the oven to 180°C/fan 160°C/gas 4. Lightly grease and line a 900g loaf tin.

Pop the butter into a large non-stick pan and heat until melted, then add the garlic and cook for a few seconds until just golden. Add the onion and cook for another 5 minutes until just soft.

Add the tomato purée, mushrooms, carrot and salt and cook for a further 5 minutes. Now add all the spices and cook for 5 minutes. Add the lentils and stock and cook on a low to medium heat for 15 minutes until the lentils are softened and all the liquid has evaporated from the base of the pan.

Take the mixture off the heat, transfer to a large bowl and leave to cool for at least 30 minutes. As soon as it is cool enough to touch, add the breadcrumbs, nuts, eggs, cheese and coriander and give it all a thorough mix until you have a really colourful mixture that is quite stiff.

Spoon the mixture into the prepped tin and push down using the back of a spoon, making sure to pack it in tightly. Bake for 50 minutes to 1 hour, then leave in the tin for 20 minutes before turning out into a small roasting dish.

Turn the grill on. Mix the yeast extract with the hot water so you have a mixture that is runny enough to brush, then add the ketchup. Brush the outside of the nut roast with the mixture and grill for just 3–5 minutes and your nut roast is ready to serve.

# kransekake biscuit tower

Serves 16    Prep 1 hour, plus chilling
Cook 40 minutes

**For the biscuit dough**

500g ground almonds

500g icing sugar, sifted

4 egg whites

1 teaspoon almond
  extract

oil, for greasing the tin

**For the icing**

3 tablespoons water or
  lemon juice

400g icing sugar, sifted

2 egg whites

1 tablespoon black
  sesame seeds

**To finish**

chocolate-covered nuts,
  seeds and wrapped
  chocolates

sugared almonds and
  edible flowers (or other
  edible decorations)

This is a Scandinavian biscuit tower that is traditionally created for special celebrations and, boy, is it special, with its rings of chewy, sweet, almond biscuit dough, stacked one on top of the other. Specialist recipes often require specialist equipment, but I have found a way of making this without needing anything fancier than a round cake tin base, a knife and the ability to cut a freehand circle.

Begin by toasting the ground almonds to really bring out their nutty flavour. Toast in a non-stick pan over a medium heat, stirring all the time, until golden. Leave to cool totally and then sift to remove any lumps. Add the icing sugar and stir until well combined.

Make a well in the centre, add the egg whites and almond extract and mix until you have a dough that comes together. If you find it's a bit crumbly, add a few drops of water until it does. Roll the dough into a flat patty, wrap and chill for at least 2 hours.

Grease and line the base of a 25cm springform tin. Take the dough out and place in the tin. Using your

→

celebration cakes

hands or the base of a heavy tumbler, push the dough in until you have a smooth, even layer that covers the base right to the edges. Remove the side of the tin, then measure a rim, 1.5cm inwards from the outside of the circle, and score a circle. Do the same again, creating another ring and then another, and so on, until you have a small circle in the centre. You should have 7 rings and 1 circle.

Preheat the oven to 200°C/fan 180°C/gas 6. Line three baking trays (or as many as you have) with some baking paper.

Take off the sides of the springform tin and gently lift away the outside ring of biscuit. Pop onto a tray. If the shape gets lost, you can just fix it or, if it breaks, just push it back together. Do this to all of the rings.

Bake for 10 minutes for the large rings, 6–8 minutes for the medium rings and 4–6 minutes for the small rings. They should be golden and will be very soft, so leave to cool on the trays for 5–10 minutes, then transfer to a wire rack to cool completely. Do this until you have baked them all.

Make the icing by adding the lemon juice or water to the icing sugar in a bowl and mixing with the egg whites. This is the type of icing that will set hard and not run everywhere – perfect for piping. Pop the icing into a piping bag, snip off a small opening and, starting with the biggest ring, pipe back and forth across the width of the ring, going all the way around. Sprinkle with the black sesame seeds as quickly as possible before the icing starts to dry. Repeat for the other rings.

It's time to stack. Take the largest ring and pipe icing on the serving board or dish so you can 'glue' the ring in place. Pop the next ring on top, using a few drops of icing to glue it, and keep doing this until you've done about three rings. Now fill the hollow in the middle with some of your chocolate-covered nuts or sweets. Add a few more rings, and again fill the middle with nuts or sweets. This cake is not traditionally filled, but I like the idea that the otherwise empty cavity is a receptacle for even more sweet delights.

Once you get to the top, secure the last piece with icing. I like to decorate with edible flowers, sugared almonds or other edible decorations, whatever the occasion calls for.

# chapter six

# BISCUITS
# & BITES

# raspberry amaretti biscuits

**Makes** about 20    **Prep** 40 minutes
**Cook** 15 minutes

butter, for greasing
the trays

4 medium egg whites

340g caster sugar

340g ground almonds

2 x 9g tubes of freeze-
dried raspberries,
blitzed to a powder

1 teaspoon almond
extract

20 small fresh
raspberries
(or see introduction)

200g icing sugar

Amaretti are a biscuit that people seem slightly afraid to make. Just because they are often found for sale in beautiful tins with crunchy cellophane and fancy bows doesn't mean they are difficult or tricky to create at home. In fact, home-made amaretti are the best, these ones in particular, which are soft and delicious and almondy, with a subtle hint of raspberry all the way through and a hidden raspberry in the centre. These too can be given as a gift. Just remind your recipients that they don't hang about and want to be eaten straight away because of the fresh fruit. If you want these to last longer you can use freeze-dried raspberries instead of fresh.

Start by preheating the oven to 190°C/fan 170°C/gas 5 and lining two large baking trays with baking paper, greasing them just very slightly to allow the paper to stick to the tray and not go flying.

Now get on to making the biscuit paste mixture by whisking the egg whites in a large clean bowl until they are firm. Add the sugar and fold through gently using a spatula or metal spoon. Add the almonds along with the blitzed-up raspberry powder and almond extract and mix thoroughly until you have an even paste.

Have the icing sugar at the ready along with the raspberries. Take a heaped tablespoon of mixture, about 40g if you want to be precise, and shape it into a flat round disc. Wrap the disc around a raspberry to form a ball shape, pinching it together underneath so that the raspberry is completely enclosed. The paste may crack a bit along the top, but don't worry.

Drop each ball into the icing sugar and roll around until fully and generously coated. Place seam-side down on the baking trays, making sure they are about 2cm apart, as they will spread just a little.

Now bake these for 12–15 minutes until they are just lightly golden. Take them out and leave to cool on the tray for 10 minutes before moving them to a cooling rack.

# rhubarb and custard butter kisses

**Makes** about 20   **Prep** 40 minutes
**Cook** 12 minutes

The classic rhubarb and custard boiled sweets don't actually taste much like rhubarb, but they are certainly distinct and unique in flavour, so I thought it would be interesting to mix them with melted white chocolate for the filling to my delicate rippled custard biscuits.

Have two baking trays at the ready, lined with some baking paper and lightly greased.

To make the dough, add the butter, icing sugar and vanilla seeds to a bowl and whisk until the mixture is really light and fluffy. Add the flour, the custard powder and the baking powder and mix until it all comes together nicely into a thick paste.

Add the food colouring to a corner of the paste and mix the paste carefully in that corner so you are colouring only a quarter. Take a clean spoon and mix the whole thing so you have uneven ripple throughout.

### For the biscuits

200g unsalted butter, plus extra for greasing the trays

50g icing sugar

½ vanilla pod, with the inside scraped out

200g plain flour, sifted

4 teaspoons custard powder

½ teaspoon baking powder

2 drops of pink gel food colouring

### For the filling

150g white chocolate, chopped or chips

40g rhubarb and custard sweets

Preheat the oven to 190°C/fan 170°C/gas 5.

Attach a medium 1.25cm open star-tip nozzle to a piping bag and gently add all the mixture. Pipe 4cm star shapes onto the prepared paper, leaving a 2cm gap in between each, as these do spread a little. Bake for 10–12 minutes, then leave to cool completely on the tray.

Make the filling by melting the chocolate and setting it aside. Crush the sweets to crumbs. I crush them so they are mostly fine with a few slightly larger pieces, but you don't want too many large pieces or the biscuits won't sandwich together.

Once the biscuits are cool, turn them over so you have the flat bases exposed. Take a half teaspoon of the melted chocolate and spread on the underside of each biscuit. Sprinkle the crushed sweets onto half the biscuits and then take the other biscuits and pop straight on top. Arrange on the tray and leave in a cool place for the chocolate to set, then they are totally ready to eat.

# chocolate, hazelnut and rosemary ladies' kisses

**Makes** 23
**Prep** 30 minutes, plus chilling and setting
**Cook** 15 minutes (20 minutes if roasting the hazelnuts)

100g chopped roasted hazelnuts

100g plain flour

85g caster sugar

100g unsalted butter, plus extra for greasing the trays

100g dark chocolate, chopped or chips

1 tablespoon dried rosemary

These are the sweetest little Italian biscuits I have ever eaten. I first tried them at an Italian restaurant, where they were just too inviting not to have one . . . and when I say one, I most definitely mean ten! The biscuits are flavoured with hazelnuts, then sandwiched with a dark chocolate that I like to lift with a little dried rosemary.

Pop the hazelnuts into a food processor. I like to buy the pre-roasted chopped ones, but if you can't find them you can roast the hazelnuts in a dry non-stick frying pan until golden, then leave to cool completely before blitzing to fine crumbs. Then, to save on washing up, make the entire dough in the processor.

Add the flour, sugar and butter and whizz until a dough starts to come together in the machine. As soon as it does, take out, wrap in clingfilm and chill for at least 1 hour so the dough can firm up.

Line and very lightly grease two baking trays.

Get the dough out of the fridge and take pinches of it, measuring exactly 8g each. I know this seems pedantic, and normally I'm not too bothered about being exact, but because here two biscuits are sandwiched together, it's important to make sure they are the same size. Roll each pinch of dough into a ball and pop onto the trays, evenly spaced out.

Put back in the fridge and chill for another hour.

Preheat the oven to 180°C/fan 160°C/gas 4.

Bake the biscuits for 12–15 minutes until they are just lightly golden brown. Take them out and leave to cool completely on a rack. As soon as they are cold, get on to that filling.

Melt the chocolate either in a bowl over a simmering pot of water or in the microwave, my preferred option for such a small amount. As soon as the chocolate is smooth and glossy, mix in the dried rosemary. The warm chocolate will activate that dried herb and bring it back to life in all its fragrant, herby glory.

Take one biscuit and dollop the smallest amount of the chocolate in the centre of the flat underside. Too much and it will spill over and you won't get that clean line in the centre. Pop another biscuit on top of the chocolate, gluing them together. Do the same to the rest.

Leave the chocolate to set for at least half an hour before eating. These can last a few months in an airtight jar – assuming you don't eat them all at once!

# speculoos spiced biscuits and crunchy spread

Makes 16  Prep 40 minutes, plus chilling
Cook 15 minutes

## For the speculoos spice mix

4 x 34g jars of ground cinnamon

42g jar of ground nutmeg

35g jar of ground cloves

33g jar of ground black pepper

28g jar of ground ginger

20g star anise, crushed to a fine powder (optional)

## For the biscuits

85g unsalted butter, softened, plus extra for greasing the trays

150g soft brown sugar

155g plain flour, sifted, plus extra for dusting

4 teaspoons speculoos spice mix

½ teaspoon baking powder

a pinch of fine salt

## For the crunchy spread

25g soft brown sugar

1 teaspoon speculoos spice mix

100ml condensed milk

10g unsalted butter, softened

1 teaspoon lemon juice

125g speculoos biscuits, this is about 7–8 biscuits

My dad used to give these biscuits to customers at his restaurant, individually wrapped and propped on the side of their coffee. I'm not big on ginger biscuits so these are my alternative: dark, crisp and spiced but not exclusively with ginger. If you're going to the trouble of making them, I highly recommend you make the spread too – it's so easy and a total must! This recipe produces a big batch of the special spice mix, but as it is so unique in flavour and not always easy to buy except at Christmas or in the Netherlands, I like to make plenty. It can be used wherever you want a spicy hit: in crumble, cakes, buttercream, smoothies, porridge, French toast, the list goes on and on.

Start by mixing all the speculoos spice mix ingredients straight into a large jar so you are ready to spice anything you want with this wonderfully special blend of spices.

Add the butter to a bowl along with the soft brown sugar. This sugar is so important to the biscuit dough, not just for the deep caramel colour, but also for the dark caramel flavour. Whisk this mixture until it is slightly fluffy and airy and a lot paler than when you first started.

Now add the flour, along with the spice mix, the baking powder and the salt and mix until you have formed a dough. If you find you have still got stray bits of flour that just won't come together and the dough is a little dry, then add a few drops of water at a time until the dough comes together. Wrap the dough in some clingfilm and flatten into a rough rectangle shape (this will help with rolling later). Leave to chill in the fridge for at least an hour.

Preheat the oven to 190°C/fan 170°C/gas 5 and line two baking trays with some baking paper, greasing them very slightly so that they stick to the trays without flying everywhere.

Once the dough is out, lightly flour the worktop and roll out the dough to a 32.5 x 20cm rectangle, just under 5mm thick. Have one of the shorter ends closest to you. Now use a fluted knife, a kid's fluted play-dough cutter or just a knife to cut it vertically into 4cm-wide strips. Cut the strips into 6.5cm-long biscuits. So we are so dividing the rectangle into 25 biscuits by making 4 vertical cuts at 4cm intervals and 4 horizontal cuts at 6.5cm intervals.

Once you have your rectangles cut, pop them onto the trays about 2cm apart, giving them some room to spread. Bake for 14–16 minutes until they are just slightly darker around the edges. Leave them to cool completely on the tray before eating, dipping and transferring into an airtight biscuit jar.

If you are making the spread, which I highly recommend, pop the sugar, spice mix, condensed milk, butter and lemon juice into a small food processor and whizz until you have a smooth paste. Add the biscuits and whizz until you have the crunch just as you like it. Spoon into a jar, place in the fridge and it will last in there for up to a month.

# pressed flower shortbread shards

250g unsalted butter, softened

110g caster sugar, plus extra for dusting

360g plain flour

semolina, for dusting

a small handful of mixed herbs and edible flowers (depending on what you can find or have growing)

Makes 30 shards   Prep 40 minutes, plus chilling   Cook 30 minutes, plus 15 minutes resting

In my opinion, shortbread rarely needs much in terms of improvement. It is a wonderful and delicious thing of buttery beauty. But if we're going to fancy it up, here is a simple and very beautiful way of doing so, especially if you have edible flowers and herbs growing in your garden.

Whisk the butter and sugar in a bowl until it is really smooth and quite light and fluffy. Add the plain flour and gently fold in until you have a smooth dough, using a palette knife or cutlery knife, and then get your hands in to form one lump of dough.

Take the dough and wrap in some clingfilm, flatten and chill in the fridge for 1 hour.

Once the dough has chilled, take out and tear off two large sheets of clingfilm. Put the dough in the centre of one sheet and the other on top. Roll out until it is a 35 x 30cm rectangle, about 5mm thick.

Have a large baking tray ready with some baking paper and sprinkle generously with the semolina.

Take off the top layer of the clingfilm and using the other sheet, turn the dough out onto the semolina layer. Pull the clingfilm off. Now dot over your flowers and herbs and push them gently into the dough. Place a sheet of baking paper on top and roll gently to push the flowers in securely. Put another baking tray on top and put back into the fridge for 30 minutes to firm up.

Preheat the oven to 160°C/fan 140°C/gas 3.

Put the tray (with the other tray still on top) into the oven to bake for 30 minutes. As soon as it is done, remove and leave like this for 15 minutes.

Now take the tray off the top and pull off the paper to reveal the beautiful flowers and herbs. Using a serrated knife and whilst the dough is still warm, cut into shards and leave to cool completely.

Once cool it should be crisp and delicious and ready to eat – if you can bear to eat something so pretty – though that never stopped me!

# onion seed biscuits

**Makes** approx. 50 (and 5 cups of masala chai) **Prep** 20 minutes plus chilling (10 minutes for the chai) **Cook** 15 minutes (1 hour for the chai)

**For the biscuits**

375g plain flour, plus extra for dusting

1 teaspoon salt

50g caster sugar

4 teaspoons onion seeds

100ml cold water

2 medium eggs, lightly beaten

50g icing sugar

**For the masala chai mix**

3 x 34g jars of ground cinnamon

28g jar of ground ginger

32g jar of ground nutmeg

26g jar of cardamom pods, seeds removed and crushed to a powder (unless you can find ground)

35g jar of ground cloves

25g jar of ground black pepper

**For the tea**

1 tablespoon masala chai mix

1 litre whole milk

5 teabags

condensed milk, to serve

These are very similar to traditional biscuits called nimki, which are technically savoury though I love them dusted in loads of icing sugar – they can be whatever you want them to be: sweet, savoury or anything in between. I only eat these one way and that is with a steaming hot cup of masala chai.

To make the biscuits, add the flour, salt and sugar to a large bowl with the onion seeds and mix well. Make a well in the centre, add the water and eggs and bring the dough together using a palette knife, then get your hands in to form a soft dough that is somewhere between a firmer bread dough and softer biscuit one.

Flatten it to a square about 2.5cm thick, wrap in clingfilm and chill in the fridge for at least 1 hour to allow the dough to rest. Meanwhile, preheat the oven to 190°C/fan 170°C/gas 5 and line two baking trays with baking paper.

Take the dough out of the fridge, put on a floured surface and roll out to a 5mm thickness. Using a 5cm round cutter, cut out circles, putting them onto the lined trays as you go. Re-roll and cut the scraps until you have used up all the dough.

Bake in the oven for 10–12 minutes until a light golden brown, being careful not to over-bake as they will harden. Leave to cool on the tray then tip into an airtight jar. Add the icing sugar and toss it around gently like the drum of a washing machine to allow the sugar to coat them. Leave in the jar ready to eat.

For the masala chai, firstly make up the mix and store in a large jar. You will have lots, so be adventurous. It's not just for tea; you can spice up all sorts of things, such as biscuits, cakes, porridge and smoothies.

For the tea, add a tablespoon of the spice mix into a pan with the milk and teabags and bring to the boil.

As soon as it comes to the boil, leave to simmer on the lowest heat for 1 hour with the lid on. The tea should be strong and rich.

Before serving add 1–2 tablespoons of condensed milk to the bottom of the cups. Strain the tea into a jug to remove some of the spice mix and the teabags, then pour the tea into each of the individual cups, making sure to stir, and that is your masala chai – plus you have enough of the spice mix left for when you want some more!

# chewy chocolate-chip cookies

225g unsalted butter

400g plain flour

¾ teaspoon baking powder

¾ teaspoon bicarbonate of soda

½ teaspoon salt

340g milk chocolate, chopped or chips

200g soft brown sugar

150g caster sugar

2 large eggs

2 large egg yolks

1 teaspoon vanilla extract

1 teaspoon almond extract

sea salt flakes, for sprinkling

> **Makes** 23  **Prep** 20 minutes, plus chilling
> **Cook** 15 minutes per batch (dough balls can be frozen and baked for 20 minutes from frozen)

These days you can satisfy your sweet/savoury tooth as quickly as nipping to the supermarket or simply dialling and ordering to your doorstep. Instant gratification has its place, but there is a joy in making something from scratch even if you can buy it from anywhere. Making a deliciously chewy, perfectly rounded, choc-chip cookie is one of life's joys, whether it's for yourself, a bake sale, baking with little ones, a distraction or just to fill a Sunday morning. So these are joy on a tray!

Start by melting the butter either in a small pan or in a medium bowl in the microwave. Leave to cool.

To another bowl add the flour, baking powder, bicarbonate of soda and salt and mix until well combined. Add the chocolate chips and mix again.

Add the sugars, eggs, egg yolks, vanilla and almond extracts to the melted butter and give the whole thing a really good mix until well combined.

Make a well in the centre of the dry ingredients and then pour in the liquid ingredients. Mix until you have

a stiff dough and the chocolate is well distributed. Chill in the fridge for 30 minutes.

Take a baking tray lined with baking paper and divide the mixture into balls of about 60g each. I'm not really into being totally exact with every cookie looking identical, but something about uniform cookies pleases me, so it's worth measuring them out. Once you have done them all, cover with some clingfilm.

The hardest bit now is leaving them to chill. You have to leave them for at least 4–5 hours, but I would recommend leaving them to chill totally overnight.

When you are ready to bake, line two baking trays with baking paper and preheat the oven to 180°C/fan 160°C/gas 4. Place about six dough balls on each tray, making sure to leave them around 5cm apart to allow room to spread. Sprinkle a little salt on each dough ball and bake for 14–16 minutes. You'll know these are ready when they are just very lightly golden brown around the edges and paler in the centre – that's the softer, chewy bit, my favourite part!

You want to leave these on the trays for at least 10 minutes before transferring them to a cooling rack, then using the trays to bake the remaining cookies.

# coffee meringue bark

**Makes** 2 large sheets   **Prep** 20 minutes
**Cook** 1 hour

butter, for greasing
   the trays

2 medium eggs,
   separated

125g caster
   sugar

2 teaspoons coffee
   granules

2 teaspoons hot water

2 teaspoons black
   sesame seeds

This gluten-free sweet treat is really easy to make. What I love is that you can play about with flavours, toppings and gel colourings to change it up, though I've kept this version fairly simple. Easy to store and equally as easy to eat, this bark doubles up as a quick decoration for cakes or cupcakes.

Add the egg whites to a large, grease-free bowl and have 100g of the sugar ready.

Preheat the oven to 150°C/fan 130°C/gas 2 and line two trays with baking paper.

Add the egg yolks to a small bowl along with the remaining 25g of the sugar. Add the coffee granules to another small bowl with the hot water and mix. Add to the egg yolk mixture and set aside.

Using a hand-held whisk or a free-standing mixer if you have one, begin whisking the egg whites until really foamy. As soon as they increase in volume, start adding the sugar a teaspoon at a time, whisking for at least 10 seconds between each addition. It's really important that all the sugar crystals dissolve so the bark doesn't leak. After each addition, stop and scrape down the sides to get any stray sugar crystals. Do this until you have stiff peaks that are glossy and shiny.

Now, whisk the coffee and egg yolk mixture until it is glossy, shiny and smooth and quadrupled in size. This mixture should be really thick, but not so stiff that it will not run off the beaters.

Divide the egg white mixture between the two trays, spreading really thin to a 30cm square. Swirl the coffee mixture all over the egg whites, then sprinkle with the sesame seeds.

Bake for 1 hour, which will give it lots of time to dry out and create a really good snap. Once the time is up, leave to cool completely. As soon as it's totally cooled, snap into shards and pop into an airtight container where they will happily keep.

# ginger
# and almond
# florentines

Makes 18   Prep 25 minutes, plus setting
Cook 15 minutes

50g unsalted butter,
softened, plus extra for
greasing the trays

50g soft brown sugar

50g golden syrup

50g plain flour

75g crystallized ginger,
finely chopped

50g sliced almonds

1 orange, zest only

200g dark chocolate

65g white chocolate

Brandy snap meets biscuit meets toffee, these are delicious to have lying about the house for a sweet treat, but even better wrapped and given away as a present. Laced with chopped crystallized ginger, sliced almonds and a hint of orange zest, they're finally dipped in chocolate to add to the party in your mouth!

Start by preheating the oven to 200°C/fan 180°C/gas 6. Line and very lightly grease three baking trays.

To make the florentines (and these are so easy I think you will be making them again), place the butter and sugar in a medium pan along with the golden syrup and heat until the sugar has dissolved and there are no more granules.

Take off the heat and add the flour, ginger, almonds and zest and mix to thoroughly combine.

Take teaspoons of the mixture and pop six equal mounds on each tray, leaving plenty of room for them to spread. Bake for 8 minutes. As soon as they are light golden in the centre and just slightly darker on the outside, they are ready to take out. They are still fragile when very hot, so will need to rest for about 5 minutes before you even think about moving them.

Have a cooling rack ready and gently, using a palette knife, take them one by one to cool on the rack. Once they have cooled completely they are ready to dip. Now, traditionally they have one side covered in chocolate, but that doesn't agree with me – where am I supposed to hold it without getting melted chocolate all over my fingers? So I like to half dip. No messy fingers and I get to taste the florentines two different ways.

So, melt the chocolates in separate bowls. Make sure to put the dark chocolate in a bowl deep enough for dipping the florentines. Add the melted white chocolate in swirls directly on top of the melted dark chocolate, then use a skewer to create swirls.

Take each round and dip half in, then pop out and leave to set on the tray with baking the paper that they baked on initially. Leave the chocolate to set and they are ready to eat!

$\rightarrow$

170

# fennel and coconut breadsticks

Makes 12   Prep 25 minutes, plus proving
Cook 20 minutes

40g desiccated coconut, plus 3 tablespoons for sprinkling

450g strong bread flour, plus extra for dusting

7g fast-action dried yeast

1 teaspoon salt

2 teaspoons fennel seeds, lightly crushed

250ml warm water (you may need a splash more)

vegetable oil, for greasing the clingfilm

1 egg white mixed with 1 tablespoon water

1 teaspoon sea salt flakes

Yes, you can buy breadsticks anywhere, but they are easy to make too, especially if you want to vary the flavours. I find making them very therapeutic – and then you get to eat your therapy. I can't think of a better way to feel chilled. These are dotted with fennel and covered with coconut. I love that they are both sweet and savoury at the same time, so you can eat them dipped in peanut butter, chocolate spread, tomato jam or onion chutney! Delicious all round.

Dust two large baking trays with the desiccated coconut.

Put the flour, yeast, salt and crushed fennel seeds into a large bowl and mix to combine. Make a well in the centre, add the water and bring the dough together using a cutlery knife. Now get your hands in and mix to get a dough ball.

Knead well for 10 minutes by hand on a lightly floured work surface or for 5 minutes if using a free-standing mixer fitted with a dough hook on a high speed.

Divide the mixture into 12 equal portions, about 60g each if we're being precise. Take each ball and roll into a long sausage shape, about 25cm long, on a very lightly floured surface. What I love about making these is the unevenness of the breadsticks – they all have the odd nodule or quirk that makes them extra special. So yes, we want them to be the same, but do we really?

Place the breadsticks on the prepared baking trays, spacing them a few centimetres apart. Cover loosely with a sheet of greased clingfilm and leave in a warm place until they have doubled in size.

Meanwhile, preheat the oven to 220°C/fan 200°C/gas 7.

Remove the clingfilm and brush the breadsticks with the egg white mixed with water. Sprinkle over the sea salt flakes and then the coconut and bake in the top part of the oven for 10 minutes. Cover the trays with foil to stop the coconut burning and bake for another 10 minutes, until golden and the coconut on the base and top is toasted golden.

Take out and leave to cool completely on the tray before eating with your chosen dip.

# spicy chickpea crispbreads

> **Makes** about 30 shards    **Prep** 20 minutes
> **Cook** 20 minutes

300g chickpea flour, sifted, plus a little extra for dusting

2 teaspoons chilli flakes

1 teaspoon paprika

1 teaspoon salt

½ teaspoon baking powder

30g ghee or butter, softened

1 teaspoon honey

85ml cold water (you may need a little more)

1 egg white mixed with 1 tablespoon cold water

2 teaspoons cumin seeds

1 teaspoon curry powder

I grew up watching my mum, very not British, eating spicy snacks with her tea. I never understood until I started drinking teas and realized how well the two go together, especially if your tea is sweet and your snack is savoury. These spicy crispbreads do not have to be eaten with tea; they are just as great used as a vehicle for cheese or chutney or instead of poppadoms. But they do work brilliantly just with a cup of tea.

Start by preheating the oven to 200°C/fan 180°C/gas 6 and having two baking trays at the ready.

Add the sifted chickpea flour into a bowl. It's important as chickpea flour has a little more moisture in it than regular flour, so is more prone to large clumps. Now add the chilli flakes, paprika, salt and baking powder and mix well to combine.

Add the ghee or butter along with the honey, and, using your hands, mix and crumble the butter in until you have no large lumps left. Make a well in the centre and add the cold water. Using a cutlery knife, mix the dough until it starts coming together. Now it's time to get your hands in and give everything a really good squeeze to bring the dough together into a

neat ball. The dough should be quite firm, but, if you find it is still quite dry, add a few teaspoons of water at a time until the dough comes together.

Divide the dough in two. Dust the work surface with a little of the chickpea flour and start gently rolling out half of the dough.

Now take a large sheet of baking paper, the right size to fit the baking trays, pop the dough on top of that and roll on that paper. This will just mean transferring will be easier. Roll as thin as possible, about 1.5mm thick, making sure to dust your rolling pin if you need to.

Pop onto the tray. Repeat with the other half of the dough, putting it on the second baking tray once rolled out. Poke the dough all over with a fork at this stage to reduce bubbling during baking.

Mix the egg white with the water, brush all over the dough and sprinkle over the cumin seeds and the curry powder. Bake for 18–20 minutes until the centre of the sheet is dry to touch.

As soon as the sheets come out of the oven, leave on the trays until they have cooled completely, giving them loads of room to dry and crisp up some more. Take the dried sheets, break up into shards and they are ready to eat any which way.

# mint choc-chip nanaimo bars

| For the biscuit base | For the mint top | For the milkshake |
|---|---|---|
| 125g unsalted butter, plus extra for greasing the tin | 100g unsalted butter, softened | 3 squares of Nanaimo |
| 50g caster sugar | 2 tablespoons whole milk | 2 scoops of vanilla ice cream |
| 40g cocoa powder | 250g icing sugar, sieved | a small handful of fresh mint |
| 1 medium egg, lightly whisked | a few drops of mint extract | 300ml whole milk |
| 200g digestives, crushed | a few drops of green food colouring | chocolate sauce |
| 100g desiccated coconut | 6 after-dinner chocolate mints, roughly chopped or broken | squirty cream |
| 50g almonds, roughly chopped | | chocolate chips or shavings |
| | | 2 sprigs of fresh mint |

**Makes** 16 bars (and 2 milkshakes)
**Prep** 25 minutes, plus chilling (10 minutes for the milkshakes)
**Cook** 5 minutes

When planning any holiday, the first thing I look at is places to eat. My kids love to do this too. When we decided to travel through Canada, we immediately went online and searched 'Things to eat in Canada'. There was a wealth of foods, but Nanaimo bars really stuck out. These have a rich chocolate base and a sweet mint custard with choc chips, because the word mint should always be followed with the words choc chip! These also make a delicious milkshake. Just saying . . .

Line a 23cm square tin with baking paper and lightly grease.

Make the base by adding the butter, sugar and cocoa powder to a medium saucepan and heating gently until the butter has melted and the sugar has dissolved. Take off the heat and leave to cool for about 10 minutes. Now add the egg and quickly mix until the mixture is quite thick. Add the biscuits, coconut and almonds and mix until everything is well coated. Put into the lined tin and press into an even layer. Pop into the fridge for 30 minutes.

Make the topping by adding the butter and milk to a bowl and whisking well. Add the icing sugar and combine using a spoon, then go back in with the whisk and beat until really light and fluffy. Add the mint extract and enough food colouring to achieve that minty colour. Finally, add the after-dinner mints and fold them through so they are evenly dispersed.

Spread the mint mixture evenly on top of the chilled base and leave in the fridge for another 30 minutes. Take out, cut into squares and these are ready to eat. They're great with a glass of milk.

To make the milkshake, add 2 Nanaimo bars to a blender with the ice cream, mint and milk and whizz until thick. Squeeze the chocolate sauce down the inside edge of two long glasses and pour in the milkshake. Top with some squirty cream, chocolate chips or shavings and then a sprig of mint. You are set!

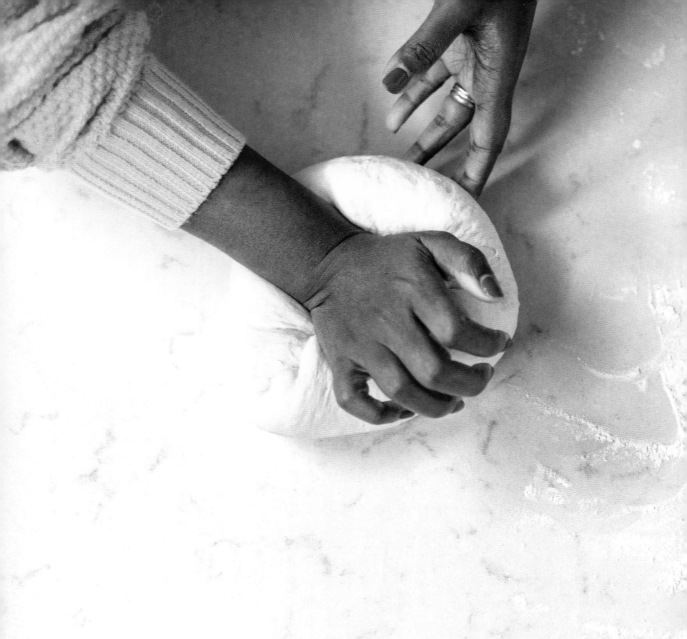

# chapter seven

# BREADS

# & BUNS

—

# cornish splits

**Makes** 9  **Prep** 30 minutes, plus rising  **Cook** 25 minutes

**For the loaves**

375g strong bread flour, plus extra for dusting

30g unsalted butter, softened, plus extra for greasing

7g fast-action yeast

2 teaspoons caster sugar

¼ teaspoon fine salt

300ml warm milk

**For the quick jam**

400g frozen strawberries, defrosted

100g caster sugar

1 lime, zest and juice

2 teaspoons cornflour

**For the filling**

400ml double cream

2 tablespoons icing sugar, plus 1 extra tablespoon for dusting

1 teaspoon vanilla bean extract

butter, for spreading

These glorious little delights are the kind of things that make me remember why I love food – because often the simplest recipes can be the most delicious. These round, yeasted loaves are split while still warm, buttered generously, filled with strawberry jam and then served with the biggest dollop of freshly whipped vanilla-laced cream! What could be better? In my mind, nothing.

Start by making the dough. Pop the flour into a bowl, add the butter and rub in until there are no more lumps. Add the yeast and sugar to one side of the bowl and then a pinch of salt to the other side.

Make a well in the centre and add the warm milk. Using a palette knife, mix the whole thing until it just comes together.

Now it's time to knead. This dough is super sticky, so this is definitely better done in a stand mixer, if you have one, using the dough hook on a medium speed for 6 minutes. If you are using your hands, make sure to dust the surface and your hands with flour, and re-flour them whenever the dough feels too sticky. Then work that dough, kneading it for about 10 minutes until it is smooth and elastic. Leave it to prove in a warm spot until it has doubled in size.

Meanwhile make the quick jam. Put the strawberries in a pan with the sugar. Add the zest of the lime. Squeeze the lime juice into a small bowl, add the cornflour and mix to a paste. Add to the pan and mix through. Put the pan on a medium heat and cook for about 5 minutes, stirring occasionally, until the mixture has thickened. Take off the heat and set aside to cool completely.

Once the dough has doubled in size, take out of the bowl and drop on to a floured surface.

Roll the dough into a sausage shape and cut into 9 equal pieces. If you want to be precise, then each one needs to be between 70 and 75g.

Pop the loaves onto a lightly greased baking tray, cover with a piece of greased clingfilm and leave to prove until doubled in size.

Preheat the oven to 200°C/fan 180°C/gas 6.

Bake the loaves for 15 minutes. As soon as they are done, remove the tray from the oven, place the buns on a cooling rack and leave to cool completely.

→

While the loaves cool, mix the cream in a large bowl with the icing sugar and vanilla, whip up to soft peaks then spoon it into a piping bag.

Once the loaves have cooled it's time to do the 'split' bit of the Cornish splits. Cut each bun on a slant starting at the top and cutting downwards, on an angle, being sure not to go all the way through or you will have a Cornish burger!

Butter inside generously on the bottom half, spoon in some of that cooled jam and then pipe in the cream.

Dust with a little icing sugar and eat straight away. No hanging around here!

# cinnamon and cocoa swirl loaf

Makes 1 loaf
Prep 35 minutes, plus rising
Cook 30 minutes

**For the bread**

500g strong bread flour, plus extra for dusting

2 teaspoons ground cinnamon

2 teaspoons fine salt

7g fast-action yeast

3 tablespoons oil, plus extra for greasing

300ml lukewarm water

**For the swirl**

2 tablespoons cocoa powder

2 tablespoons caster sugar

**For the paste**

1 tablespoon strong bread flour

1 teaspoon cocoa powder

½ teaspoon fast-action yeast

a pinch of salt

1 tablespoon caster sugar

1 tablespoon oil

1 tablespoon water

salted butter, to serve

The dough itself here is very simple and perfect if all you want to do is make a basic loaf, but I always think why not add frills if you can? I, for one, like a frill, a tassel and a fringe, so that is what this distinctive loaf is all about. The dough is laced with fragrant cinnamon and swirled with sweet cocoa. It has a distinctive look and a lovely chewy top.

Start with the dough. Put the flour in a mixing bowl, add the cinnamon and salt on one side, and the yeast on the other. (Keeping them separate prevents the salt killing the yeast.) Add the oil and give it all a stir. Make a well in the centre and pour the water into it.

If you're using a mixer, attach a dough hook and mix till the dough forms a ball. If you don't have a mixer, bring the dough together by hand.

Now the dough needs kneading until it is smooth, stretchy and elastic. If you are doing this by hand, lightly flour the worktop and knead for about 10 minutes. If you are using a mixer, knead with the dough hook on a medium speed for 6 minutes.

Pop the dough into a lightly greased bowl, cover with greased clingfilm and leave to prove in a warm spot until doubled in size.

Once it has risen, knock the air out of the dough by punching straight into the bowl. Tip it out onto a lightly floured surface.

Have a 900g loaf tin greased and ready. Roll the dough out to a 40 x 25cm rectangle. Mix the cocoa powder and sugar in a bowl and sprinkle all over the dough.

With the shorter end closest to you, begin rolling the dough up, pulling just a little as you do so, to get the roll really tight and close. Pinch the seam together to stop the filling from escaping. Tuck in the ends underneath, making sure the seam is on the base.

Drop the roll into the loaf tin, cover with the same greased clingfilm and leave to prove till doubled in size again.

While that happens, make the paste by mixing the flour, cocoa, yeast, salt, sugar, oil and water together.

Preheat the oven to 220°C/fan 200°C/gas 7. As soon as the dough has doubled in size, take off the clingfilm and gently brush the paste all over the surface of the loaf. Be generous.

Bake for 25–30 minutes, then take out and leave to cool completely in the tin.

Now it's time to slice and spread with delicious cold, salted butter – the only real way to enjoy this beauty.

breads & buns

# cherry chelsea buns

Makes 12  Prep 30 minutes, plus rising and soaking
Cook 20 minutes

**For the buns**

450g strong bread flour, plus extra for dusting

50g unsalted butter, chopped into small pieces

14g fast-action yeast

50g caster sugar

1 teaspoon fine salt

1 teaspoon ground nutmeg

1 medium egg, beaten

150ml warm milk

up to 75ml water

**For the cherry filling**

200g dried cherries (or mixed berries and cherries, if that's all you can find)

300ml boiling water

1 teaspoon almond extract

25g unsalted butter, softened

25g caster sugar

12 glacé cherries

**For the sugar glaze**

100g caster sugar

30ml hot water

These buns are similar to those sold by that well-known Scandinavian furniture store, where I always wish they would put the cafe at the start, before the endless row of arrows, so I could grab something to sustain me throughout. Saying that, the buns do always help ease the blow at the end when I've bought more than I meant to! The buns here have no cinnamon in sight, as the dough is flavoured with nutmeg instead, with a sour cherry swirl through the centre, a crisp, sweet, sugary glaze and, like all wonderful things, finished with a cherry on top.

Pop the flour and butter in a bowl and rub in. Add the yeast, sugar and nutmeg to one side and the salt to the other. Mix well and make a well in the centre.

Mix the egg and milk in a jug and pour into the well. With a palette knife, mix the ingredients to bring the dough together. If it is very dry and not coming together, add a few drops of water until it does.

Knead for 10 minutes by hand on a floured surface, or for 6 minutes on high using a machine with a dough hook. Leave in a warm place covered with greased clingfilm or a wet tea towel, until doubled in size.

To make the filling, put the dried cherries in a bowl with the boiling water and leave for at least 1 hour or until the fruits are soft, plump and fully rehydrated. Then drain the water off and squeeze them a handful at a time to remove all moisture. Pop them into the food processor along with the almond extract, butter and sugar and blitz to a smooth paste.

Now make the buns. Have two large baking trays ready, lined and lightly greased.

Dust the worktop with some flour. Take out the dough and roll out to form a rectangle of 25 x 45 cm.

With the longer side closest to you, spread the filling all over, right to the edge. Roll up from the longer edge into a log. Cut into 12 equal slices and pop them onto the lined trays, leaving lots of room around them to prove and rise. Using the palm of your hand, squash them down a little to flatten out and allow them to prove evenly. Cover with greased clingfilm and leave to prove until doubled in size again.

Preheat the oven to 180°C/fan 160°C/gas 4. Pop a glace cherry in the centre of each proved bun and bake for 20 minutes until golden and puffed up.

Meanwhile, make the glaze by mixing the sugar and hot water. Once the buns are baked and still hot, brush the glaze all over them, to get a lovely sheen.

These are perfect eaten with a hot beverage or, better still, popped in a paper bag and stuck in your pocket for any intensive shopping experience!

# brioche custard buns

## For the brioche

375g strong white bread flour, plus extra for dusting

1 teaspoon fine salt

7g fast action yeast

175g unsalted butter, chilled

4 medium eggs,

whole milk, chilled

## For the chocolate anise crème patissière

250ml whole milk

3 whole star anise

4 egg yolks

100g caster sugar

1 teaspoon vanilla bean paste

20g cornflour

20g cocoa powder

20g unsalted butter

## To finish

1 egg beaten, to glaze

sugar pearl nibs or sprinkles, for decoration (optional)

1 x 220g can of peach slices

---

**Makes** 10  **Prep** 40 minutes, plus rising
**Cook** 35 minutes

---

I'm a big fan of brioche and can eat it every which way, but these buns are the way I like to eat it best: sweet, soft brioche dough, filled with a chocolate custard, just kissed with the shine of star anise and topped with a juicy slice of peach. The buns look delicate, but they are satisfyingly heavy to hold and something about this contrast makes me smile. I love a weighty sweet treat and these are that while being light and sophisticated too.

Mix the flour, salt and yeast in a large bowl. Grate the butter straight into the flour mixture and mix through so that the separate pieces of butter get covered.

Crack the eggs into a measuring jug and lightly beat till they are just broken. Now add enough milk to make up 250ml of liquid – you might only need a splash or two. Make a well in the centre of the dry ingredients, pour in the egg mixture and mix using a palette knife till the dough begins to come together.

Now knead for 10 minutes on a floured surface, or, if you are using a mixer, knead with a dough hook for 6 minutes (I would highly recommend a mixer if you have one because this is quite a sticky dough). The dough should become firmer and elastic, and you should see streaks of butter all the way through.

Pop the dough back into a bowl and put in the fridge to rise for 2 hours or until doubled in size.

Now make the crème patissière by putting the milk and star anise in a pan. Pop onto a high heat and bring to a rapid boil, till it's just scorched the milk, then take off the heat.

In another bowl, whisk together the egg yolks, sugar, vanilla, cornflour and cocoa powder till you have a really thick mixture.

Remove the star anise and slowly and gradually pour the warm milk into the egg mixture, just a small amount at a time, whisking between each addition, until it is all incorporated.

Now pop the mixture back into the milk pan and place on a medium heat, whisking all the time. It should take about 3½ minutes to get a really thick chocolate crème pat.

Remove from the heat and whisk in the butter, then transfer into a bowl and cover with clingfilm, making sure it touches the surface of the mixture to prevent it forming a skin. Once it's cooled for 10 minutes, pop into the fridge.

When the dough has doubled in size, place on a lightly floured worktop and divide the dough into 10 equal-sized dough balls. If you are being precise each one should be 75–80g.

Have a deep muffin tray at the ready. On the floured worktop, roll each mound into a 12cm circle, about 0.75cm thick. Pop the circle of dough into a hole in the muffin tray. Push your thumb down into the dough to create a little cavity in which to place the chocolate crème pat. This will create some overhang, but that is perfect.

Do this to the other 9, then cover with a sheet of greased clingfilm and leave to prove for 20 minutes.

Preheat the oven to 180°C/fan 160°C/gas 4. Scrape the cooled crème pat into a piping bag, or you can just spoon the mixture into the buns. If you need to loosen it (which you may), mix thoroughly with a spoon till it's smooth and glossy again.

Brush the edges of the brioche cups with the beaten egg and, optionally, sprinkle sugar pearl nibs (or your favourite sprinkles) all over the edges. Pipe or spoon the crème pat into each cavity, then pop a slice of peach right on top.

Bake for 25 minutes, till the edges are golden. Once baked, leave them in the tin for 20 minutes before removing. These are equally delicious warm or cold, and perfect for breakfast, brunch or any time of the day, really.

# citrus polonaise buns

Makes 14
Prep 50 minutes, plus rising
Cook 35 minutes

## For the bread

500g strong bread flour, plus extra for dusting

175g unsalted butter, very soft

1 teaspoon salt

7g fast-action yeast

1 lemon, zest only, saving the juice for the curd

1 orange, zest only, saving the juice for the curd

4 medium eggs, lightly beaten

a few splashes of whole milk

100g mixed peel

## For the citrus curd

juice of the lemon and orange as above

150g caster sugar

2 tablespoons cornflour

3 medium egg yolks and 1 whole egg (save the whites for the meringue)

100g butter, softened

## For the meringue

150g caster sugar

3 large egg whites (or 180ml if you're using egg whites out of a carton)

¼ teaspoon fine salt

¼ teaspoon cream of tartar

These little beauties are my take on the French classic brioche polonaise. They consist of light butter brioche laced with mixed peel, sliced and filled with a citrus curd (rather than the traditional crème pat), then covered in meringue and a sprinkling of almonds and lightly toasted until golden. I admit they are not quite authentic, but I like these flavours, so I threw it all up in the air to come up with something I could call my own.

Start by making the dough. Add the flour to a large mixing bowl or the bowl of a free-standing mixer.

Add the butter and, using your hands, rub the butter into the flour until there are no large chunks left. Add the salt to one side of the bowl and the yeast to the other. Now add the orange and lemon zests and give everything a really good mix.

Put the eggs into a measuring jug and lightly beat, add enough milk to bring the amount of liquid up to 250ml (you don't need to add any extra liquid if you are already at 250ml).

Make a well in the centre of the flour mixture, and pour the liquid into it. If you are doing this by hand, bring the dough together, lightly dust the surface of your worktop with flour and knead the dough until smooth and stretchy, which will probably take about 10 minutes. If you are using a free-standing mixer, attach the dough hook and knead for 6 minutes on a medium speed. Finally, briefly knead in the mixed peel. Roll the dough into a neat mound, pop into a lightly oiled bowl covered with greased clingfilm and leave to prove in the fridge for 2 hours.

You can make the curd while you wait. Juice the lemon and orange straight into a saucepan. To the pan add the sugar, cornflour, egg yolk, egg and butter and whisk through until thoroughly combined.

→

Pop the pan onto a medium to low heat and whisk constantly until the mixture is really thick. This should take a few minutes. As soon as it's thick, take off the heat and transfer into a bowl. Cover it with a sheet of clingfilm touching the surface to stop a skin from forming and leave to cool.

You can use this time to make the meringue. Add the sugar, egg whites, salt and cream of tartar to a heatproof bowl. Set it above a pan half-full of boiling water. Make sure the base of the bowl doesn't touch the water, or you will have scrambled egg.

Pop onto the heat and stir for about 3 minutes on a medium heat until the sugar has dissolved.

Now using an electric hand whisk and with your thermometer at the ready, whisk on a high speed until the temperature of the mixture is between 68 and 72°C, this can take up to 10 minutes.

As soon as it has reached the required temperature, take the pan off the heat and keep whisking the mixture until the bowl is just warm to the touch and the peaks are stiff. Leave to cool completely, cover and place in the fridge.

Once the dough has finished proving, turn it out onto a floured work surface.

Line a baking tray with some baking paper.

Roll the dough to a 1cm thickness and using a 7cm fluted cutter, cut out 14 rounds and set them on the tray.

Cover with some greased clingfilm and leave to prove for 15 minutes.

Preheat the oven to 220°C/fan 200°C/gas 7, remove the clingfilm and pop the tray in. Bake for 12–15 minutes.

Take out of the oven and leave to cool completely.

Slice each one across the middle like a scone, spread with the curd and sandwich together. If your curd has developed any lumps, just push the mixture through a sieve to get rid of them.

Once you have filled them all, take a bun, and spoon equal amounts of the meringue on top of each bun and use the back of a spoon to create peaks. Once coated, leave it on the tray and repeat with the rest. If the meringue is too thick to dip you could also use a spatula or the back of a spoon to cover the bun.

Now, to finish these off, use a blowtorch to toast the tops, or pop them under a grill – making sure to watch them carefully all of the time. These won't wait, so enjoy straight away!

# msemmen pancakes with a pistachio and mint honey

| **Makes** 10 | **Prep** 40 minutes, plus resting |
| :--- | :--- |
| **Cook** 40 minutes | |

**For the pancakes**

385g plain flour

¼ teaspoon salt

1 teaspoon baking powder

1 tablespoon caster sugar

1 medium egg, lightly beaten

300ml lukewarm water

1l bottle of vegetable/sunflower oil for greasing and cooking

50g semolina for sprinkling

**For the pistachio and mint honey**

50g pistachios

2 tablespoons oil

3 teaspoons dried mint

340g jar of clear honey

I first came across these online, when I saw a video of someone eating them. They didn't look like naan or chapati, maybe vaguely like a paratha, but they were surely a staple from somewhere and I had to know where. Eventually, I found a recipe for this wonderful Moroccan pancake-like pastry. I'm still unsure how to pronounce the name, but who cares how you say it when these delicious square pan-cakes are so good. I have yet to visit Morocco, but these chewy, flaky, golden treats make me want to book a flight right now.

Add the flour, salt, baking powder and sugar to a large bowl and combine. Crack in the egg and mix through, then add the water, a little at time until it comes together to form a dough.

Lightly grease the worktop and knead the dough by hand for 5 minutes. If it starts to stick, alternate between greasing your work surface and greasing your hands. Oiling both will make for a slippy slide situation. The dough should be smooth and elastic and that's how you will know it is ready. Have a baking tray at the ready, very lightly greased. Oil is so important in this recipe.

Cover your hands in oil – be very generous – and give the dough ball a good smothering of oil too. Now take out chunks of dough and make sure they are well covered in grease. If you're being precise, each ball has to be around 60–65g, but whatever the size you should have 10 dough balls, equal or otherwise.

Flatten each piece of dough onto the work surface then fold the edges in towards the centre, bit by bit, until you have a rough ball. Turn it over so it is seam-side down, then cup your hand over the top of it and rotate it so that the dough is being rolled between your palm and the work surface to make a smooth ball. Pop on the greased tray, pinched side down. Leave to rest covered with a damp tea towel for 15 minutes.

Have the semolina ready in a bowl with a teaspoon in it.

Grease the worktop, then take a dough ball and, using your hand, press it flat until you have a round sheet of dough, almost transparent enough to be able to see through. Be careful not to tear holes in it; it's easily done.

Sprinkle a light dusting of semolina all over, then fold the bottom third up over the middle third of the dough. Sprinkle with more semolina. Bring the top third down over the folded dough and sprinkle with semolina again. What you should have created is a long rectangle, made up of three layers of pastry.

Working from the short end, from left to right fold one third of the dough over the middle third. Sprinkle with semolina. Then, from right to left, fold the remaining third over the top. What you should be left with now is a square. If not, don't panic, it will still be delicious. Pop it back onto the tray and do the same with the rest, until you have completed them all.

Lay the tea towel back on top and leave to rest for 15 minutes.

Meanwhile, make the pistachio and mint honey by adding the pistachios to a food processor with the oil and blitzing till you have a smooth paste. Then add the mint and honey and whizz until it all comes together. Pop back into the jar (or your serving dish) and set aside. This should keep for up to a month stored in a jar, but it won't last, because you will finish it with these flaky, chewy beauties. I promise.

Now to make the msemmen: grease the worktop lightly (I told you there was a fair amount of greasing involved in this recipe), pop one square down and, using a rolling pin, roll till the square is at least three times the size, about 15 x 15cm. Repeat with all of them and pile them back on the tray. They are oiled enough to not stick to one another, don't worry.

To cook, pop a small glug of oil into a non-stick frying pan on a medium to high heat. All our cookers are different so you will get a feel for what is right once you cook the first one.

Add the msemmen and cook for 3 minutes on one side then flip over and cook for a minute on the other. They should puff up slightly whilst cooking and have dots of golden brown all over.

Repeat with all the msemmen and leave them wrapped in the tea towel to keep them soft and warm.

To eat, smother with the pistachio and mint honey and roll. They are best served with a hot steaming cup of mint tea.

# honeycomb rolls

Makes 13
Prep 35 minutes, plus rising
Cook 25 minutes

**For the bread rolls**

400g plain flour, plus extra for dusting

100g natural yoghurt

2 tablespoons caster sugar

¼ teaspoon fine salt

7g fast-action yeast

200ml lukewarm water

oil, for greasing the work surface

**For the honeycomb**

200g caster sugar

60g golden syrup

2 teaspoons bicarbonate of soda

**For the honeycomb filling**

125g mascarpone

50g white sesame seeds

2 tablespoons tahini

**For the topping**

1 tablespoon butter, melted

1 teaspoon white or black sesame seeds

These are traditionally known as honeycomb rolls because of the way they are laid out: sweet little buns misaligned by one, to create a honeycomb effect. But with such a great name, I couldn't resist incorporating actual honeycomb somehow. So I've filled them with mascarpone sweetened with a bittersweet honeycomb dust, with a hint of tahini for nuttiness, then covered in more of that delicious honeycomb and finally dusted with sesame seeds. If you don't want to make the honeycomb yourself, you could use that famous chocolate bar with its perfectly thin chocolate edge, but I think you should give the home-made stuff a try, especially if you never have before, because you'll find it's surprisingly easy.

To make the honeycomb, put the sugar in a large pan along with the golden syrup. This magical stuff expands really quickly, so you do need a decent-sized pan. Have a baking tray lined and greased, ready for the honeycomb to be poured onto. Prep is key here – molten sugar allows no dilly-dallying! Have your bicarbonate of soda ready measured beside you along with your whisk and a heatproof spatula.

Pop the pan onto a medium to high heat. Stay close, and be ready to reduce the heat or even take the pan off the heat if need be.

Stir the sugar and syrup to gently combine. It should begin to sizzle and the sugar should start to melt. Don't mix the whole time, just occasionally. You will see the sugar around the outside start to go darker first – that's when you should give it a little stir and encourage the darker sugar to mix with the lighter.

→

Take off the heat as soon as the mixture is an even deep-amber colour (if you have a sugar thermometer, the temperature should have reached 150°C). This should take somewhere between 3 and 4 minutes.

Tip the bicarbonate of soda in and use your whisk to whisk it in fast – no time to wait here. Honeycomb waits for no man! It should start to really puff up and take over your pan like some 1980s horror movie goopy ghoul! Take the whisk out once all the bicarbonate of soda has been incorporated and use the spatula to pour and scrape it all out into the lined baking tray and leave it to expand by itself. Leave it to cool for at least 2 hours while you get on with the rest of the recipe. Don't be tempted to touch it – your fingertips will thank me later!

Meanwhile make the bread dough by adding the yoghurt to the flour in a bowl and use a palette knife to roughly combine them. Now add the sugar and salt to the bowl on one side and the yeast to the other side. (This is to stop the salt killing the yeast.) Give it another good mix. Make a well in the centre and add the water. Use the same knife to bring the dough together.

Generously dust the work surface with flour, and bring the dough together on it until it is no longer too sticky. Knead for 5 minutes.

After 5 minutes, grease the work surface with oil and knead again for another 5 minutes. The dough should be smooth and a little more elastic. Put it into a greased bowl, cover with a damp tea towel and leave to prove until doubled in size.

Meanwhile, to make the filling, measure out 50g of the honeycomb and roughly crush it. Combine it with the mascarpone, sesame seeds and tahini.

Line a small baking tray with some greaseproof paper and lightly grease.

Knock the air out of the dough and tip it onto a flour-dusted work surface.

Tear mounds off the dough until you have 13 equal pieces (about 55g each). Using the palm of your hand, squash down until you have a flat round piece of dough ready to be filled. Do this to all of them.

Take the filling mixture and add a heaped teaspoon to each bit of dough, making sure to divide it evenly, until you have used up all the mixture.

Take a circle of dough, pick it up and bring the edges into the centre to enclose the filling, pinching as you go. Be sure to give it a really good pinch so that the filling doesn't ooze out. It still might even after your efforts, but that's OK. Repeat with all the dough.

Pop them pinched-side down on the tray, leaving just a small gap to allow the buns to expand whilst proving, and lay them out in honeycomb style.

Cover with a wet tea towel or greased clingfilm and leave to prove for 30 minutes.

Preheat the oven to 200°C/fan 180°C/gas 6 and bake the rolls in the oven for 15 minutes until they are wonderfully golden.

Meanwhile, melt the butter. Measure another 50g of honeycomb and roughly crush it. When the rolls are baked, get the tray straight out onto a cooling rack and brush them immediately with the hot melted butter, then be generous with the honeycomb and sesame seeds. Doing this while they are still hot is essential for the honeycomb to melt and stick to the buns.

Leave to cool for at least 30 minutes before eating. I love to have these with a steaming-hot cup of tea but it has to be builder's alongside something as sweet and gooey as this. The remaining unused honeycomb can be kept in an airtight container.

# salmon and dill stuffed focaccia

**Makes** 1 large sheet / Serves 8 as a side
**Prep** 30 minutes, plus rising    **Cook** 30 minutes

Focaccia is by far one of my favourite breads. Although it's easy to buy, it's also easy to make and the texture of freshly baked focaccia is like nothing else. The chewy, airy bread is just the best, but made better with every bite when you get a flood of really good oil. In this case I am using clarified butter, because it has a flavour like no other, and infused with the garlic it's just out of this world. This focaccia is so much more than just a layer of bread, too, because before baking it is filled with delicious smoked salmon and dill.

### For the dough

500g strong bread flour

2 tablespoons clarified butter

2 teaspoons salt

14g fast-action yeast

350–375ml lukewarm water

semolina for dusting

oil for greasing tray

### For the filling

100g smoked salmon

a small handful of fresh dill, finely chopped

1 teaspoon ground black pepper

### For drizzling

100g clarified butter

2 cloves of garlic, peeled and thinly sliced

a sprinkle of sea salt flakes

Put the flour into a large mixing bowl, add the butter and quickly rub it in with your hands until it has disappeared totally into small crumbs. Now add the salt on one side of the bowl and the yeast on the other. Give it all a quick mix, then make a well in the centre and add all the liquid, then use a palette knife to bring the dough together as much as possible.

A mixer with a dough hook is best for kneading this, as the dough can be a little sticky and I hate it when most of it ends up on my hands. If you are kneading by hand, make sure to lightly dust both the work surface and your hands with flour at the start and again whenever it feels too sticky. Whatever method you choose, knead the dough for 10 minutes until smooth, stretchy and elastic. Keep adding small amounts of flour if it keeps sticking, but not too much. Put it in a lightly greased bowl, cover with greased clingfilm or a wet tea towel and leave to prove until doubled in size. The time can vary depending on the warmth of the place you put it; you will find the perfect spot for proving, the more you bake.

While that is happening, get the clarified butter for the drizzle into a pan over a high heat. As soon as it starts to smoke, add the sliced garlic, then remove the pan from the heat. The butter should be hot enough to really brown that garlic, so now leave it all to infuse and allow the butter to cool.

Prepare a large baking tray (about 20 x 30cm) with a light layer of oil and sprinkling of semolina. Tip the dough out onto the tray, generously oil your hands to stop it sticking to you, then encourage and spread the dough out into the corners. Cover one half with the smoked salmon, and sprinkle on the dill and the ground black pepper. Take the other half of the dough and fold it over to encase that lovely filling. Turn the dough so it fits comfortably in the centre of the tray. Using your hands again push that dough all the way out into the corners. Now, cover with some greased clingfilm or a wet tea towel and leave to prove until doubled in size again.

Preheat the oven to 220°C/fan 200°C/gas 7.

Use your fingers to poke dents all over the dough. It may feel a little weird, but it also feels a little good! Don't press all the way through the dough, but just enough to create great big indents where your garlicky clarified butter will sit.

Once you have done that, drizzle over the melted butter, reserving the garlic slices to use later. Make sure the butter fills all those dents. It may look like an awful lot, but don't worry, the dough wants it and will absorb it all, making for the most delicious focaccia, I promise, so go for it.

Bake for 20–25 minutes until golden brown.

Take the focaccia out, give it a good sprinkling of salt and scatter the browned garlic slices over the top.

Leave to cool before eating, as this will encourage the oils to absorb right back in.

This is perfect as a side for a main dish, but I really enjoy this on a picnic, because it's a delicious chewy bread with a delicious filling all set to go.

# rose
# harissa
# rugelach

**For the harissa**

5 tablespoons coriander seeds (about 30g)

5 tablespoons cumin seeds (about 40g)

5 tablespoons fennel seeds (about 40g)

5 tablespoons chilli flakes (about 30g)

10 heads of organic roses, petals removed

2 whole bulbs of garlic, peeled

1 medium red onion, peeled and chopped

1 large red pepper, de-seeded and chopped

1 tablespoon salt

100ml olive oil

**For the rugelach**

160g self-raising flour, plus extra for dusting

a pinch of salt

120g chilled butter, roughly cubed

120g full-fat cream cheese, chilled

1 egg for glazing

black pepper

butter or oil for greasing baking tray

→

> **Makes** 12 (harissa makes 520g and will keep in fridge up to 2 weeks or freezer up to 3 months) **Prep** 40 minutes, plus resting **Cook** 45 minutes

My favourite episode of *The Apprentice* is when the contestants have to drive all about town to find obscure items. One year they had to find rugelach, and before anyone even failed that challenge I was off researching these little beauties. A Polish, bready, but almost short bake that is layered with chocolate and then rolled up to look like little croissants – they're delicious yet dangerous, because I can eat about ten in one sitting. For this recipe, however, I have replaced the chocolate with home-made rose harissa. The flavour is spicy yet sweet, with the fiercest of reds twirled in that short, creamy pastry. You can easily replace the harissa with more traditional flavours, but this is one worth trying.

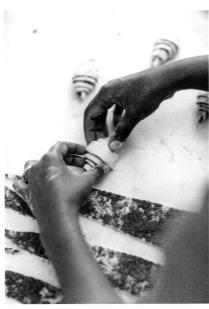

For the harissa, add the coriander, cumin and fennel seeds to a non-stick pan and toast on a high heat until they begin to pop.

Add all the harissa ingredients, except the oil, to a blender and whizz everything together to a smooth paste. If you find the mixture too stiff, add a few spoons of extra oil to help it along.

Add the oil to a pan, add the paste and cook on a low heat for 15 minutes, until it is dry, rich and thick. Transfer to a jar and set aside to cool completely.

Now for the rugelach. Put the flour and salt into a food processor. Add the butter and whizz until you have large buttery clumps. Next, add the cream cheese and whizz until the mixture comes together into a large ball. Wrap and chill for 1 hour to firm up the dough. Prepare a baking tray by lining it with some lightly greased baking paper.

Tip the dough, which can be quite sticky, out onto a generously floured surface. Roll it into a rectangle of 35 x 25 cm. Take 2 heaped tablespoons of the harissa and spread it all over the pastry. With the longest side facing you, cut the rectangle into 6 equal vertical strips. Then cut each strip on the diagonal, starting at the bottom and going all the way up to the opposite corner to create a triangle. Do this to each strip, which will give you 12 triangles in total.

Taking one triangle at a time, and with the widest part of it closest to you, roll gently towards the point – you should end up with what look like sweet little croissants. Place on the tray with the little point of the triangle underneath, so it doesn't just pop up. Repeat this with all the triangles. Place them a little distance apart, but these don't spread or grow much so don't be worried if you have a smaller tray. Put into the fridge to chill for 30 minutes.

Pre-heat the oven to 180°C/fan 160°C/gas 4.

Take the tray out of the fridge, brush the rugelach all over with some beaten egg and dust with a little cracked black pepper. Bake in the oven for 25–30 minutes, until they are light, crisp and golden brown amongst the fiery red.

Leave to cool completely before eating, or at least try!

# pulled chicken doughnuts

**Makes** 12  **Prep** 35 minutes, plus rising and chilling
**Cook** 40 minutes

### For the bread

550g strong bread flour, plus extra for dusting

175g unsalted butter, softened

60g caster sugar

1 teaspoon fine salt

14g fast-action yeast

4 eggs, lightly beaten

100ml cold water

1½ litres of oil, to deep fry

### For the chicken filling

1 large chicken breast or 2 small – around 280g

7 tablespoons barbecue sauce (125g)

3 tablespoons mayonnaise (60g)

1 teaspoon chilli flakes

1 small handful of fresh chives, finely chopped

### For the savoury dust

1 teaspoon garlic granules

1 teaspoon ground cumin

1 teaspoon salt

1 teaspoon caster sugar

1 teaspoon dried coriander

Doughnuts filled with chicken, need I say more? But seeing as you're here and I have your attention, I will. These doughnuts are filled with a quick-cooked shredded chicken, then fried and covered in a delicious savoury-sweet dust. If anyone didn't know these were savoury, they could be fooled. This recipe is worth a try just to see the confusion and delight on people's faces.

Start by making the dough. Put the flour in a bowl, add the butter and rub in until there are no big butter chunks remaining.

Now add the sugar and salt to one side of the bowl and the yeast to the other side. Mix thoroughly and then make a well in the centre. Mix the eggs and water in a jug, then pour into the well and mix with the dry ingredients until the dough roughly comes together.

If you are kneading the dough by hand, flour the work surface and knead for 10 minutes until the dough is stretchy and shiny. But I prefer to do it using a mixer, as the dough is quite sticky and buttery.

When using a dough hook on a mixer it only needs kneading for 6 minutes on a medium speed.

Leave to prove in a warm place covered with a wet tea towel or greased clingfilm.

Meanwhile, make the filling by boiling the chicken breast in a small pan of water on a medium heat for 15 minutes until the meat is cooked through.

Once cooked, lift the chicken out of the water and leave on a plate until it's cool enough to handle. Use two forks to shred and pull it apart. Now add flavour to your chicken by adding the barbecue sauce, mayo, chilli flakes and chives and giving it all a good mix around. Cover and set aside in the fridge.

Once the dough has doubled in size, tip out onto a floured work surface. Roll the dough into a sausage shape and cut out 12 equal portions of around 90g each. Making them the same size is important if you want them to fry evenly.

Have a lined and greased baking tray at the ready. Roll out a dough ball to about 12cm diameter. Add a tablespoon of chicken mix, not heaped, into the

→

centre. Gently lift up the edges of the dough from all around the sides and seal the chicken inside, pinching firmly in the centre. Pop it on the tray, pinched side up.

Do this to the rest of them, then pop the tray into the fridge for 1 hour.

In the meantime, make the dust by mixing the garlic, cumin, salt, sugar and coriander.

Just before the hour is up, add the oil to a medium-sized pan. Make sure the oil is not higher than halfway up the sides. Heat the oil on a medium heat – if you are using a thermometer you want the oil to reach 150°C. But if not, you can drop a piece of bread into the oil and if it sizzles and rises to the top, the oil is ready.

Prepare a baking tray lined with kitchen paper to drain the doughnuts on.

Gently place a doughnut into the oil, pinched side up. Don't overcrowd the pan, just do three at a time.

Cook the doughnuts gently for 6 minutes until golden brown all over. You don't need to turn them, just occasionally push them down into the oil using a slotted spoon. When ready, take out and pop onto the paper to drain, then pop in the oven for 10 minutes to finish cooking through, removing the kitchen paper first. While still piping hot, sprinkle with the savoury dust. Do the same to all of them, frying and sprinkling.

Allow to cool down, then eat them lukewarm, or even totally cooled. All I can say is: you are welcome!

# cheat's sourdough

| | |
|---|---|
| **Makes** 1 large loaf | |
| **Prep** 30 minutes, plus rising | |
| **Cook** 30 minutes | |

This ingredients list is in two parts, as the making of this spans over 24 hours. I mean, there is being ready with everything weighed out, but so far in advance would be too much to ask.

**1st set of ingredients**

200g strong bread flour

200ml water

7g fast-action yeast

**2nd set of ingredients**

400g strong bread flour

200ml water

7g fast-action yeast

1 teaspoon salt

Many a sourdough starter has come and gone in my house, but none has remained long enough for me to hand it down to anyone! With eighteen tropical fish, four laying hens, a budgie called Rayf and a rabbit called Cornelius, when we go away my neighbours have their hands full enough in keeping our little zoo alive, so I can hardly ask them to also tend to my sourdough (which is always named Julio, said with a Spanish accent. Julio the Sourdough!). So no starters here – this is my cheat's version. The dough sours overnight and is ready to bake after 24 hours sitting in the warm.

Decide when you want to eat your fresh bread. I tend to begin the recipe between 6 or 7 a.m. on a Saturday, so I can knead, prove, bake and eat 24 hours later.

I like to start by using the bowl that I will later knead my dough in, which for me is always the bowl of my free-standing mixer. Or simply use a large bowl. Add the first set of ingredients (flour, water, yeast) to the bowl and give the gloopy liquid a really good mix. Cover with a wet tea towel and leave in a warm spot for 24 hours to bubble away and sour gently.

Now it's time for the second set of ingredients, so add the flour, water, yeast and salt to the bubbling dough.

Attach a dough hook to your mixer and mix until the dough comes together. When it forms a ball, turn the mixer up and knead on a medium speed for about 6 minutes. If you are doing it by hand, knead on a floured surface for 10 minutes, until it's smooth, stretchy and elastic.

It's best to prove this in the pot you will bake it in. Find a large, 5-litre cast-iron pan (or a normal saucepan, but make sure it doesn't have a plastic handle as it needs to go in the oven), and line with a large piece of baking paper, pushing it to the base and around the sides. Tuck the edges of the dough under itself so you have a nice round smooth mound. Pop into the pot, add the lid and leave to prove for about 30 minutes or until it has doubled in size.

Preheat the oven to 220°C/fan 200°C/gas 7. As soon as the dough is ready, cut a few slashes in the top and pop the pan into the oven with the lid on. Bake for 30–40 minutes. Letting it bake this way creates steam which gives a nice crust.

Once it is out of the oven, take off the lid and leave the loaf to cool completely in the pot. Then take out, slice and eat – your way! I like butter and salt, then I move on to butter and jam, then butter and cheese, and then I repeat, till there is no bread left.

# mashed potato flatbreads with egg butter

**For the flatbreads**

400g cooled mashed potato (use leftovers, buy ready-made, or even use instant mash!)

1 medium egg, lightly beaten

150g plain flour

½ teaspoon salt

2 teaspoons onion seeds

oil, for greasing

**For the egg butter**

3 medium eggs, boiled and cooled

125g butter, softened

½ teaspoon onion salt (or normal salt if you can't find any)

1 teaspoon ground black pepper

2 teaspoons dried parsley

**Makes** 6   **Prep** 30 minutes   **Cook** 20 minutes

These are a great alternative to flour flatbreads. They are soft, delicious and very simple. Perfect for when you have leftover mash you need to use up, or when you want to try something different. They are subtly spiced with delicious onion seeds and topped off with a butter that has been mixed with eggs – the butter melts and leaves behind that wonderful, rich, crumbled egg.

Start by making the flatbread dough. Put the mashed potato in a bowl, add the egg and mix together. Add the flour, salt and onion seeds and mix it all in really well until you have dough that feels more difficult to mix as it stiffens.

Preheat the oven to 220°C/fan 200°C/gas 7. Line two baking trays with greaseproof paper and lightly grease.

Generously oil your hands and divide the dough into 6 equal pieces. If you want to be precise, each one should be around 100g.

Still with very greased hands, roll the dough mounds into balls. The mixture is still quite soft, so take your time. Pop three onto each tray and, using the palm of your hand, press into circles with a diameter of roughly 12cm. Prick all over the surface of the circles to stop them from puffing up.

Bake for 20 minutes. They are ready when the outsides are golden but the centres are still soft.

Meanwhile, make the egg butter by adding the boiled eggs, butter, onion salt, pepper and parsley to a food processor and blitzing until you have a smooth, eggy mixture.

Take the flatbreads out of the oven and leave them wrapped in a clean tea towel to keep them warm and soft.

When you are ready to serve, spread with lashings of the egg butter. Any leftover egg butter will keep in the fridge for up to 3 days.

# onion pretzels

500g strong bread flour,
plus extra for dusting

7g fast-action yeast

25g caster sugar

30g crispy fried onions

1 tablespoon onion
granules

2 teaspoons dried chives

50g unsalted butter,
melted, plus extra
for greasing the trays

300ml warm water

3 tablespoons
bicarbonate of soda

**To finish**

1 medium egg, lightly
beaten

1 teaspoon paprika

1 teaspoon onion
granules

1 teaspoon salt

**Makes** 12   **Prep** 45 minutes, plus rising
**Cook** 25 minutes

Pretzels are surprisingly easy to make and these ones are even easier because, instead of the usual intricate shape, I just do knots. Laced with crispy onions and chives and then topped with a dusting of intense onion flavour, they are soft and yummy and super satisfying.

Start by adding the flour to a large mixing bowl with the yeast, sugar, onions, onion granules and chives and mix until well combined.

Add the butter and mix through using a cutlery knife. Make a well in the centre. Add the water and mix until the dough comes together.

Attach the dough hook to a free-standing mixer and knead for 5 minutes on medium until the dough is smooth and stretchy. Cover and leave to double in size.

Grease two baking trays. Take the dough out and divide into 12 equal-sized balls, about 75g each. Roll out each ball to a 30cm sausage shape and then tie into a knot (see photo overleaf), tuck the ends underneath and pop onto the greased trays. Leave covered with greased clingfilm for just 15 minutes.

Preheat the oven to 200°C/fan 180°C/gas 6.

Bring a large saucepan of water to the boil. Add the bicarbonate of soda, stir in well until dissolved, then leave to simmer. Gently drop in a few of the dough knots (just enough so they don't touch) and cook for 10 seconds. Flip with a slotted spoon and leave in for another 10 seconds.

Drain and pop back onto the greased tray. Repeat with the rest. Glaze them with the beaten egg. Mix the paprika, onion granules and salt together, sprinkle all over the knots and bake for 12 minutes. Take out, leave to cool a little on a rack and eat while they are still warm.

→

# cardamom lemon iced fingers

**Makes** 12    **Prep** 25 minutes    **Cook** 15 minutes

**For the fingers**

500g strong bread flour, plus extra for dusting

14g fast-action yeast

50g caster sugar

2 teaspoons fine salt

4 tablespoons sunflower oil

7 cardamom pods, seeds removed and crushed, or 2 teaspoons ground cardamom

zest of 2 lemons

2 medium eggs, lightly beaten

150ml warm water

150ml warm milk

**For the icing**

400g icing sugar

5 tablespoons lemon juice, from the zested lemons

The first time I tried iced fingers was when I found them reduced in the supermarket with a yellow sticker calling to me! At 12p a pack, how could I not? The bag was slightly torn, the bread was slightly stale, but those things aside, I thought their sweet icing and fragrant nutmeg-kissed flavour was simply delicious. Here I have created my own version with a few little differences. These are fragrant with cardamom and lemon zest, while the juice of the lemon is used to make a super-sweet and equally tart icing.

Start with the dough. Put the flour in a large mixing bowl. Add the yeast and sugar to one side of the bowl and the salt to the other side. Add the oil, cardamom seeds and lemon zest and give it all a mix.

In a jug, mix together the eggs, water and milk. Make a well in the centre of the dry ingredients and pour in the liquid.

Now it's time to knead. This is a wet, sticky dough, so I highly recommend using a stand mixer or hand mixer with a dough hook, on a medium speed. By hand it will take longer and you'll need to flour the work surface and your hands as you go along.

Knead until the dough is smooth, shiny and very elastic, then place in a lightly greased bowl, cover with greased clingfilm or a wet tea towel and leave to prove in a warm place until doubled in size. As it proves you should be able to smell the cardamom.

Once the dough has doubled in size, tip it out onto a floured surface. Knock out all the air.

Have a greased tray at the ready. Divide the dough into 12 mounds. Each roughly 75g, if you're being precise. Roll each one into a sausage shape about 10cm long. Place them on the tray with gaps of about 2cm between each one. Pop a greased piece of clingfilm on top and leave to prove again until they have doubled in size. As this happens, they will just touch and then can be baked in a batch.

Preheat the oven to 200°C/fan 180°C/gas 6. Once the buns have proved, bake in the oven for 10–15 minutes, then leave to cool on the tray.

Make the icing by mixing the icing sugar and lemon juice together to a smooth paste. Once the buns have cooled completely (this is important, or the icing will just run off), tear off a bun and dip the top side in the icing until it is covered, scraping off the excess. Do the same to the rest.

These are best eaten as soon as you can, while the bread is still really soft and fresh.

# chapter eight

# SAVOURY BAKES

# seekh kebab toad in the hole

**For the seekh kebab**

500g lamb/beef mince

1 small red onion, very finely diced

a small handful of coriander, chopped

2 tablespoons garam masala

1 tablespoon gram flour/ cornflour

1 teaspoon salt

1 medium egg

**For the tray**

90g clarified butter

1 tablespoon coriander seeds, crushed

2 medium red onions, quartered

1 medium red pepper, cored and cut into 8 chunks

2 tomatoes, quartered

**For the batter**

140g plain flour

½ teaspoon salt

2 medium eggs

175ml whole milk

**Serves** 4   **Prep** 30 minutes, plus chilling
**Cook** 50 minutes

This is toad in the hole, Asian style! I'm a big fan of the original, but even with my favourite recipes sometimes I like to mix things up and do what I call 'desi style', so instead of sausages this contains meatballs, made from mince that's spiced gently and cooked with chunks of onions, then enveloped in a simple Yorkshire pudding-type batter.

Start by making the seekh kebab mixture. Add the mince to a bowl with the onion, coriander, garam masala, flour, salt and egg, then get your hands in and mix the whole lot together until you have an even mixture.

Divide into 12 equal mounds. Using wet hands, create small even neat rounds, pop them onto a plate and leave to chill in the fridge while you prep the rest of the recipe.

Preheat the oven to 220°C/fan 200°C/gas 7. Put the ghee into a medium ovenproof roasting dish (about 25 x 30cm) and pop into the oven to melt. This should only take 5 minutes.

Drop in the coriander seeds, onion, red pepper and tomatoes, mix through, then return to the oven to cook for 10 minutes. The perfect time to make your batter.

Add the flour to a bowl with the salt and mix. Make a well in the centre, add the eggs and milk then, using a whisk, bring the thick batter together.

Take the roasting dish out of the oven and carefully place the kebabs in it. Put back into the oven for 10 minutes – just enough to seal the mince.

Take the tray out again and gently reposition everything so there are 3 kebabs per portion and all the veg are nicely placed, before pouring in the batter.

Bake for 20–25 minutes. The batter will puff up and envelop the kebabs as it cooks. Leave for 10 minutes before serving.

# baked chilli churros

**Makes** approx. 40–45    **Prep** 40 minutes
**Cook** 20 minutes    **Best eaten** fresh
(but sauce can be made up to 24 hours ahead)

**For the churros**

400ml water

200g unsalted butter, roughly chopped

200g strong bread flour, sifted

2 teaspoons paprika

approx. 2 teaspoons chilli flakes, depending on how spicy you like it

4 medium eggs, lightly beaten

100g mature Cheddar cheese, finely grated

1 egg, lightly beaten

2 teaspoons onion salt

2 teaspoons dried chives

**For the tomato dip**

9 small tomatoes, skins removed (about 600g)

3 tablespoons olive oil

1½ teaspoons onion seeds

¾ teaspoon onion salt

¾ teaspoon sugar

1 large clove of garlic, crushed

Can I still call these churros if they are baked instead of deep fried, and savoury instead of sweet? I think so. Whatever they are, they're delicious.

Begin by making the dough for the churros. Add the water to a small non-stick pan along with the butter and pop on to a high heat. Bring to the boil and as soon as the butter has melted, remove from the heat.

Now add the flour, paprika, and chilli to a bowl and mix thoroughly.

Quickly tip the flour mixture into the water/butter mixture and beat vigorously until you have a smooth, even paste. Pop the pan back onto a low heat and continue to mix until you have a dough that is just coming away from the sides.

Take off the heat and give it a vigorous stir to cool it down, which should take about 2 minutes.

Add the eggs, a little at a time, making sure to stir well between additions. It might look lumpy and separated, but will come together as you keep mixing, so persevere.

Keep adding until all the eggs are used up.

Now pop the dough into a separate bowl to cool completely. Once it has, add the grated cheese and mix well, then put it in a piping bag. I like to use a large star tip nozzle, because it creates texture which gets crunchy in the oven, but you could also use a plain one. Preheat the oven to 220°C/fan 200°C/gas 7 and prepare 3 trays lined with some baking paper.

Pipe lines on the trays, approx. 7cm long, leaving a gap of 1cm in between to give them room to expand.

→

Do this until you have piped all the mixture, then brush gently with the beaten egg and sprinkle over the onion salt and dried chives.

Pop the trays into the oven and bake for 23–25 minutes, making sure to move them around halfway through so everything bakes evenly.

Meanwhile, you can get on with making the tomato dip, which couldn't be simpler. Pierce each tomato with the tip of a knife – this will make them easier to peel later. Put the tomatoes in a small pan with enough water to fully immerse them. Pop onto a high heat and boil for 1–2 minutes.

Take off the heat, drain, and as soon as they are cool enough to handle, gently remove the skins.

Chop them up, seeds and all, and leave to one side.

Add the oil to a small pan. As soon as it is hot, add the onion seeds. When they pop, add the salt, sugar and garlic, cook for a few seconds and then drop in the chopped tomatoes and cook on a low heat until any excess liquid has evaporated and the mixture has thickened up – this can take about 5 minutes.

Put into a serving dish.

Take the churros out of the oven and leave them on the tray for 20 minutes before moving them, then transfer onto a serving dish and they are ready to eat with the tomato dip.

# saag paneer spanakopita

<table>
<tr><td>

**For the filling**

750g spinach

60g ghee/clarified
butter, or regular
butter, plus extra
for greasing

1–4 teaspoons chilli
flakes, depending
on how hot you
like it

1½ tablespoons
cumin seeds

</td><td>

225g paneer, grated

6 cloves of garlic,
crushed

2 small onions,
finely diced

1½ teaspoons salt

100g ricotta

1 medium egg, lightly
beaten

a handful of
coriander, chopped

</td><td>

a handful of chives,
chopped

**For the pastry case**

270g filo pastry,
defrosted if frozen

100g ghee/clarified
butter/unsalted
butter, melted,
to brush

2 tablespoons
sesame seeds

</td></tr>
</table>

Serves 4  **Prep** 30 minutes
**Cook** 50 minutes

Saag paneer (a dish of spinach and paneer cheese) is one of my favourite things to eat. It's not a dish I grew up with, as cheese doesn't feature often – if ever – in Bangladeshi cuisine, but as our family expanded and mixed and my palate became ever more adventurous, it's something I loved to order when we ate out, especially if it wasn't a halal eatery, as paneer was always a good, textured alternative to meat. This recipe fuses it with a spanakopita, the classic Greek filo pastry pie. Thanks to the pastry, no chapatis are required; it's an all-in-one kind of situation.

Start by making the filling. Add the spinach to a large bowl, pour boiling water all over it and use a spoon to dunk all the leaves under the surface. Leave to wilt for 5 minutes.

Drain and rinse under cold water and, as soon as it is cool enough to handle, squeeze out as much moisture as you physically can. Chop then finely slice the clumps of spinach, before leaving to one side.

Now add the ghee to a non-stick frying pan. As soon as it is hot, add the chilli flakes and cumin seeds and heat gently until the seeds begin to pop.

Add the paneer and cook for 5 minutes until you start to get some golden colour on it. Add the garlic and onions and cook for 5 minutes until the onions are soft.

Add the salt and spinach and cook until there is no moisture at all left at the base of the pan.

Take off the heat and leave to cool totally. As soon as it has, add the ricotta, egg, coriander and chives and mix through. Set aside.

Preheat the oven to 190°C/fan 170°C/gas 5. Grease the inside of a 20cm square cake tin.

Brush a sheet of filo all over with ghee and pop it into the centre of the greased dish, leaving overhang on two sides.

Get another sheet, brush it with ghee, then pop it into the tin as before, making sure that this time the overhang is on the other two sides.

Do the same with another sheet, but this time place it in the tin at an angle, and do the same with another sheet adding that on the opposite angle.

What you should have now is the dish lined with filo, and with overhang on all the sides. Grease your three remaining sheets of filo and put them to one side while you put the cooked filling into the dish and flatten the top.

Fold the overhanging pastry edges up and over the top, ruffling them gently as you do. Now take each of the extra sheets, crumple them up and place them gently on top until the filling is entirely covered. Sprinkle over the sesame seeds.

Put into the oven and bake for 30–35 minutes until the filling is hot and the pastry is crisp and golden. Leave for 15 minutes before eating.

# pepperoni pull-apart

Serves 6
**Prep** 30 minutes, plus resting
**Cook** 25 minutes

**For the dough**

400g self-raising flour, plus extra for dusting

1 tablespoon dried oregano

1 tablespoon caster sugar

1 teaspoon salt

7g fast-action yeast

300ml warm water

**For the filling**

4 tablespoons sriracha sauce (or chilli/tomato sauce of your choice)

80g thinly sliced

pepperoni, about 16 slices

8 cheese slices of your choice

8 basil leaves

3 tablespoons olive oil for brushing, plus extra to grease the tin

With all the flavours of a pizza, this is perfect for when you want more than just a regular slice of bread with your soup. It's very simple to create, but looks and tastes like you have made a real effort. Best of all, it's great for sharing, which is exactly the kind of food I love to eat.

Begin by making the dough. Add the flour, oregano, sugar, salt and yeast to a large bowl, or the bowl of a stand mixer, making sure to keep the salt and yeast on separate sides until you begin. Then mix everything together.

Make a well in the centre, add the water and mix the dough until it starts to come together.

Now either flour a work surface and knead the dough by hand, or attach a dough hook and knead in the stand mixer. If you are doing it by hand it should take about 10–12 minutes of continual kneading. If you are doing it by machine, 6 minutes on a medium speed should do the trick.

What you are looking for is a stretchy dough that is smooth, shiny and still just a little bit tacky.

Once it is ready, cover the bowl with greased clingfilm and leave the dough to prove until doubled in size.

Generously grease the inside of a 900g loaf tin with oil.

As soon as the dough has risen, tip it out on to a flour-dusted work surface and roll it out to a rectangle 25 x 35cm.

Brush the top with the sriracha, distribute the 8 squares of cheese evenly over the top, dot with a few slices of the pepperoni and pop a basil leaf on top of each.

Now cut the rectangle into 8 equal squares. Take each square and fold it in half like a book. Stack them side by side in the tin with the filling bit exposed at the top. Then leave, covered in greased clingfilm, to prove until it has doubled in size again.

Preheat the oven to 200°C/fan 180°C/gas 6.

Once it has risen enough, take off the clingfilm and bake for 25 minutes.

Take it out of the oven and brush all over with olive oil, then leave in the tin for 20 minutes before pulling apart and tearing and sharing!

# polenta bake

Serves 6
**Prep** 25 minutes, plus chilling
**Cook** 50 minutes

**For the polenta**

1 litre of water

225g polenta

½ teaspoon salt

½ teaspoon turmeric

2 teaspoon ground black pepper

50g unsalted butter

50g mature Cheddar cheese, grated, plus an extra 100g for the top

oil for greasing and brushing polenta

**For the sauce**

397g can of evaporated milk

200ml whole milk

200g mature Cheddar, finely grated

1 tablespoon cornflour

a pinch of salt

300g baby spinach leaves

120g salmon trimmings

The first time I tried polenta this way, it was the kind you can buy already set in a block, packaged in plastic and ready to slice. I probably didn't read the instructions properly, because it didn't turn out very well, or I did follow the instructions and it was just a lost cause. It doesn't have to be, as this is the kind of thing you can make yourself and set in advance, ready to be baked when you get home for tea. Mixed with cheese, it's a delicious alternative staple to potatoes or rice, especially if you're looking for something a bit different to mix your meals up.

Let's make the polenta first. Grease and line a 900g loaf tin with some clingfilm.

Add the water to a pan and bring to the boil. Put the polenta in a bowl with the salt, turmeric and pepper and mix until evenly combined. Now, in a steady stream add the polenta mixture to the boiling water, turn the heat down and mix. Keep stirring until you have a mixture that is really stiff and begins to come away from the pan.

Now add the butter and the cheese and mix until combined.

Tip the mixture out into the prepared loaf tin and flatten the top. Leave until cooled slightly and then chill in the fridge for about 4 hours, until firm.

Now start to make the cheese sauce by putting the evaporated milk into a small non-stick pan along with the milk. Stir and bring to the boil, then turn the heat down completely. In another bowl, mix the cheese with the cornflour until the cheese is coated. Tip it into the milk mixture, along with the salt, and mix until you have a thick, cheesy sauce. Take off the heat.

Preheat the oven to 200°C/fan 180°C/gas 6. Oil the base and sides of a baking dish (approx. 25 x 30cm).

Take the polenta mixture and cut into 1cm slices and lay them on the baking dish. It doesn't have to be an even layer, they can overlap a bit, it's fine. Lightly grease the top by brushing with olive oil and pop into the oven for 20 minutes to lightly crisp up the polenta.

Remove from the oven and pile the spinach right on top. Sprinkle over the salmon trimmings and pour over the sauce, then sprinkle over the extra grated cheese.

Place in the oven and bake for 30 minutes, until you have a delicious crisp, cheesy top. Leave for 10 minutes before eating.

# cauliflower cheese lasagne

Serves 6    Prep 30 minutes    Cook 1 hour

butter, for greasing

500g mascarpone

2 tablespoons garlic granules

1 medium onion, finely diced

1 teaspoon salt

1 teaspoon ground black pepper

100ml whole milk

350g red leicester cheese, grated

a large handful of chives, chopped

2 small cauliflower heads, excluding stalks, thinly sliced (approx. 800g)

1 broccoli head, excluding stalk, thinly sliced (approx. 300g unprepped weight)

6 fresh lasagne sheets (½ a pack)

This does what it says on the tin. It's cauliflower cheese crossed with lasagne, that's it. So if you like both of those things, which I definitely do, then this one is for you, all for you.

Have a deep lasagne dish ready (25 x 20 x 8cm). Grease the inside with some butter. Preheat the oven to 180°C/fan 160°C/gas 4.

Start by making the filling. Add the mascarpone to a large bowl along with the garlic granules, onion, salt, pepper and milk and mix through. Now add 200g of the cheese and the chives and stir to combine well.

Add the sliced cauliflower and broccoli to a microwaveable bowl with a tablespoon of water. Cover with clingfilm and cook for 7–8 minutes, until just soft.

You may have to do this in two batches as there is rather a lot of veg. Add the cooked vegetables to the mascarpone mix, making sure not to add any excess liquid from the dish. Stir through.

Take a third of the mixture and spread evenly in the base of the lasagne dish. Add 3 lasagne sheets on top in a single layer to cover all the cauliflower mix, cutting them if necessary to make them fit.

Add the next third, cover with 3 lasagne sheets again and then add the rest of the cauliflower mix.

Sprinkle with the remaining grated cheese and bake in the oven for 45 minutes, until the top is toasted and the centre is piping hot. Just before serving, switch to grill mode, to get some colour on that lasagne top.

# tarragon mushrooms and eggs on toast

Serves 6    Prep 15 minutes
Cook 25 minutes

**For the mushrooms**

6 tablespoons oil

3 cloves of garlic, crushed

1 medium onion, grated to a paste

6 portobello mushrooms, caps intact, stalks removed and chopped

½ teaspoon salt

1 teaspoon ground black pepper

300ml double cream

a small handful of fresh tarragon, leaves chopped, or a tablespoon of dried

70g breadcrumbs, fresh or dry

6 medium eggs

**To serve**

6 slices of toast

chopped chives

This is such a simple but hearty meal: quick, easy and veggie too! Perfect for a delicious lunch, a lazy supper or any kind of brunch, the mushrooms are cooked gently in the oven, covered in creamy tarragon sauce and then topped with an egg and some breadcrumbs, before being baked again, ready to eat on crunchy toast.

Preheat the oven to 200°C/fan 180°C/gas 6.

Start with a roasting dish that is large enough to house 6 portobello mushrooms.

Add the oil, garlic and onion to the dish and mix well with your hands. Drop in the chopped mushroom stalks and mix them in too.

Finally, add the mushroom cups and, using your hands again, give them a gentle mix to coat them in all that lovely flavour.

Sprinkle with salt and pepper and mix again. Position the mushrooms so the undersides of the cups are facing upwards, then pop them into the oven to bake for 15 minutes.

Take the mushrooms out of the dish, add the cream and tarragon to the dish and stir. Return the mushroom cups and crack an egg into each one. You will find the egg will spill over, but that is totally all right. Sprinkle all over with breadcrumbs. Don't worry about the bread-crumbs getting everywhere, it helps to thicken the sauce. Season again.

Bake for 10 minutes more. If you don't like a runny yolk, bake for a further 5–6 minutes.

Place a mushroom and egg on top of each piece of crunchy toast and be sure to dish up some of that delicious creamy sauce, too.

Sprinkle with chopped fresh chives before serving.

# salt-and-pepper baked chicken and chips

Serves 4    Prep 40 minutes
Cook 2 hours

**For the chicken**

1 small chicken, halved, skin on (1.4kg)

100ml whole milk

juice of ½ a lemon

1 teaspoon salt

1 teaspoon turmeric

100g plain flour

½ teaspoon salt

2 teaspoons black pepper

**For the chips**

1 kilo small waxy potatoes, quartered lengthways

50ml oil, plus extra to grease roasting tin

4 large cloves of garlic or 8 small, peeled and thinly sliced

3 teaspoons chilli flakes, or less if you prefer

3 teaspoons ground black pepper

1 small red onion, thinly sliced

3 teaspoons sea salt flakes

This is 'salt and pepper' of the kind you get at a Chinese takeaway. As for chips from the Chinese, they may not be authentic or traditional, but they do them pretty well. So why not – especially when these ones are baked in the oven, making them easier and a little better for you than any from a deep fryer. Crisp chicken and spicy potatoes – sometimes that is all we need!

Add the chicken halves to a large pan of water, bring to the boil and boil for 10 minutes. Take off the heat, drain and leave to cool.

Now start making the buttermilk: add the milk to a bowl large enough to fit the chicken halves. Squeeze in the lemon juice and add the salt and turmeric. Mix and leave on one side for 10 minutes.

Once the chicken is cool, put it in the bowl with the buttermilk and smother it all over – get your hands right in there.

Parboil the potatoes for 15 minutes. Remove from the heat and drain.

Put the oil into a non-stick pan and, as soon as it is hot, add the garlic and cook for a minute or two until the slices just catch a little colour.

Take off the heat and add the chilli flakes, black pepper, onion and salt, then stir to coat with the hot oil.

Add the parboiled potatoes and set aside.

Preheat the oven to 200°C/fan 180°C/gas 6.

Take a large roasting dish and drizzle in a little oil. If you don't have a large one, you might need to bake in two tins – so half a chicken and some chips in each tin.

Add the flour, salt and pepper to a plate and mix.

Take the chicken out of the buttermilk mix and place face down into the flour, making sure the flour coats any part that is covered with chicken skin. Put the pieces on the baking tray skin-side up.

Scatter the potato mix all around the chicken, then cover the tray with foil and bake for 1 hour before removing the foil and cooking for a further 30 minutes.

Take out of the oven and leave to cool slightly before serving.

# baked ratatouille

**For the mince layer**

oil for greasing

250g passata

500g lamb mince

1 beef stock cube, crushed to a powder

3 garlic cloves, crushed

2 tablespoons dried parsley

150g dried breadcrumbs

**For the ratatouille layer**

3 large green courgettes, about 400g, thinly sliced into 2–3mm rounds

3 medium red onions, thinly sliced into 2–3mm thick slices

6 large tomatoes, about 500g, thinly sliced into rounds

3 small aubergines, about 600g, thinly sliced into 2–3mm rounds

3 x 125g mozzarella balls, thinly sliced into rounds, well drained and patted dry

**For the oil**

50ml olive oil

1 clove of garlic, crushed

1 teaspoon dried oregano

a sprinkling of ground black pepper

a sprinkling of salt

**To serve**

50g Parmesan, finely grated

crusty bread

---

Serves 4
**Prep** 45 minutes
**Cook** 1½ hours

---

I like ratatouille because of the way it is cooked: slowly and usually all in one pot. This is a ratatouille made pretty: layered with mince on the base and the beautiful vegetables on top, then smothered with oil and perfectly baked. All in one and delicious. Dinner's in the oven.

Preheat the oven to 180°C/fan 160°C/gas 4.

Grease the base and sides of a baking/roasting dish (25 x 30 x 5cm).

Pour the passata into the roasting dish with the mince. Add the crushed stock cube, garlic and dried parsley and mix thoroughly, then bake in the oven for 30 minutes until the mince is cooked through.

Remove from the oven (leave it switched on) and sprinkle the breadcrumbs over the mince.

Layer your slices of vegetables alternating between the courgettes, onions, tomatoes, aubergines and mozzarella, until you have finished the lot and covered the meat and breadcrumbs completely.

In a small pan, gently heat the oil. Add the crushed garlic and heat until the garlic begins to sizzle. Take off the heat, add the oregano and stir well.

Brush the top of the layered veg with the warm oil and when you have used it all up, sprinkle generously with the salt and pepper.

If you are making this in advance you can pop it in the fridge overnight until you are ready to bake. When ready, bake in the oven for 50–60 minutes, then sprinkle a light layer of grated Parmesan over the top and you are ready to go.

# teriyaki chicken noodles

**For the teriyaki sauce**

300ml hot water

30g soft brown sugar

150ml dark soy sauce

30g ginger, not peeled, finely grated

6 cloves of garlic, crushed

1–2 teaspoons chilli flakes (optional, or adjust to your taste)

5 boneless chicken thighs

225g instant vermicelli noodles (5 nests)

**To finish**

a small handful of coriander, chopped

3 spring onions, thinly sliced

1 large red chilli, sliced

sesame seeds, black and white

---

> **Serves** 5    **Prep** 25 minutes, plus marinating
> **Cook** 35 minutes

Any meal that produces as few dishes as possible to wash at the end I consider a success. Minimal washing-up, maximum smiles and even more 'mmms': these are my measures of a great recipe. This spicy, zingy, teriyaki noodle dish is exactly that – made with chicken thighs and all baked together in one roasting dish, it always results in lots of 'yums', not to mention the question, 'Did you just bake noodles?' Yes, I did. And when I say zingy, I do mean hot, so adjust the heat by taking out or reducing the chilli to your preference.

Begin by making the marinade. Mix the hot water and the sugar in a medium roasting dish, stirring to allow the sugar to melt and the water to cool. This should only take a few minutes.

Add the soy, ginger, garlic and chilli and mix well.

Next, add the chicken and leave to marinate for 30 minutes. You don't have to marinate at all if you are in a rush, but if you are cooking for the next day, then marinate in the sauce overnight and this will really soak into the chicken. Even a few hours will make a difference, if you have the time.

Preheat the oven to 200°C/fan 180°C/gas 6.

Bake the chicken for 25 minutes, until cooked through.

Take the chicken pieces out of the roasting dish, leaving the marinade behind. Add the 5 nests of noodles, flipping them over to coat them in the liquid. If your marinade has become quite dry, you can add up to another 300ml of hot water.

Put a piece of chicken back on top of each noodle nest and then put back into the oven for 10 minutes to allow the noodles to absorb all that moisture.

Take out and garnish with the coriander, spring onions, red chilli and sesame seeds, and your chicken noodles are ready to eat.

# peach-baked salmon

**For the green beans**

oil, for greasing

3 x 170g packs of French beans

50g flaked almonds

**For the salmon**

850g side of salmon, skin removed

420g can of peaches, drained (250g)

¼ teaspoon cloves

1 teaspoon garlic granules

½ teaspoon salt

½ teaspoon ground black pepper

65g toasted golden breadcrumbs

**For the dressing**

50ml olive oil

25ml balsamic vinegar

2 fresh peaches, diced

**Serves** 6–8  **Prep** 25 minutes
**Cook** 25 minutes

I often cook a whole side of salmon when I have people coming over; it feels lovely to be able to place something quick, easy and delicious in the centre of the table. I am always holding out for leftovers for lunch the next day, but too often that is not the case. This fish is simple – lightly spiced with a clove and peach sauce, baked on a bed of delicious roasted French beans and almonds, and dressed with balsamic and fresh peaches.

Preheat the oven to 200°C/fan 180°C/gas 6 and have ready a roasting dish that can comfortably fit the salmon.

Drizzle some oil on the base of the dish. Halve the green beans and drop them straight in.

Add the almonds, then, using your hands, combine them really well and flatten to an even layer.

Place the salmon right on top.

Add the drained peaches to a food processor, along with the cloves, garlic, salt and pepper. Whizz to a smooth paste.

Add the breadcrumbs and whizz very briefly again to combine.

Spoon the mixture in an even layer all over the top of the salmon, before putting it in the oven to bake for 25 minutes.

Make the dressing by adding the oil and balsamic to a bowl that's suitable to use a stick blender in. Add 2 tablespoons of the diced peaches and whizz to a smooth dressing. Add the remaining cubes of peach to the dressing and mix really well.

As soon as the salmon is done, place it gently on a serving platter.

Arrange the green beans around the side of the fish. Drizzle the dressing all over the beans and salmon and you are ready to eat.

# baked rice and eggs

**For the rice**

300g basmati rice

140g unsalted butter, melted

1 teaspoon salt

1 teaspoon ground turmeric

2 teaspoons white pepper

1 lemon, zest and juice

400g frozen green beans

600ml hot water

**For the eggs**

6 medium eggs

3 spring onions, chopped

a small handful of coriander, chopped

a pinch of salt

paprika for sprinkling

**Serves** 6   **Prep** 20 minutes
**Cook** 1 hour 45 minutes

This recipe goes against everything I was taught about rice: that it is always cooked on a stove top and never in an oven, even a fancy rice dish like a biryani, which is placed in a massive pan (I'm talking large enough to fit a grown human) and precariously set against all four hobs, heat on the edges but not in the centre. It's always a juggling act, but no one ever deployed the oven. So why not? Let's do it. For anyone nervous about cooking rice, with this recipe you needn't be, as it's simple, easy and all done in the oven, for a great taste with no worries.

Preheat the oven to 180°C/fan 160°C/gas 4.

Start with a serving dish 21 x 21cm. Glass is ideal so you can see the rice cook, but use whatever you have at home. Add the rice to the dish.

Mix the melted butter with the salt, turmeric and pepper and stir together until totally combined.

Add the zest of the lemon and mix through. Add this mixture to the rice and combine well.

Spread your frozen green beans evenly on top of the uncooked rice. Now pour the hot water carefully on top, making sure not to disturb the peace. Cover with foil and bake in the oven for 30 minutes.

Take off the foil and bake for another 30 minutes uncovered.

Meanwhile, break the eggs into a bowl, add the spring onions, coriander and salt and mix through really well.

When the rice comes out of the oven, squeeze the lemon juice all over it and drop in the egg mixture. Sprinkle generously with paprika and bake again, uncovered, for 15–20 minutes until the eggs are cooked.

Take out and leave to stand for 5 minutes before digging in.

# spiced squash strudel

**For the filling**

3 tablespoons oil

2 tablespoons coriander seeds, crushed

3 cloves of garlic, crushed

500g prepared butternut squash, diced into small cubes

1 lemon, zest and juice

½ teaspoon salt

½ teaspoon ground cinnamon

1 teaspoon paprika

50g cashews, roughly chopped

50g currants

a large handful of coriander, leaves chopped

500g puff pastry block

1 egg, beaten

sea salt

---

**Serves** 6   **Prep** 30 minutes, plus cooling
**Cook** 1 hour 30 minutes

---

I do love a classic apple strudel, but a savoury variety can be just as delicious, especially as the leftovers can be eaten cold afterwards. This one is made simply with ready-made puff pastry and filled with a spiced butternut squash mixture.

Start by making the filling, because it needs to cool before the strudel can be assembled.

Add the oil to a large non-stick sauté pan and, as soon as it is hot, add the coriander seeds. When they begin to sizzle, add the garlic and cook for about 2 minutes until golden brown.

Add the squash and stir to coat in the garlicky oil.

Add the lemon zest and juice, plus the salt, cinnamon and paprika and mix through. Pop on a low heat, put the lid on and lower the heat and leave to cook until there is no liquid left and the squash is totally soft, this should take about 40 minutes.

Take off the heat and add to a bowl to cool. Squash using the back of a fork.

Add the cashews, currants and coriander and mix through. Leave until totally cooled.

Take your puff pastry block and roll into a rectangle 25 x 20cm and pop onto a baking sheet lined with some baking paper and leave to chill in the fridge for 15 minutes.

Preheat the oven to 200°C/fan 180°C/gas 6 and put a tray into the oven to heat up.

Take the pastry out and place with the shortest side closest to you. Brush the edges with egg.

Add the filling down the centre, in the middle third of the pastry. Fold over one third and then the other third. You should have a seam running down the centre. Seal the ends. Now gently tip the strudel over so the seam is on the base.

Brush all over with the egg, make a small slit in the centre to allow steam to escape, sprinkle with salt and bake for 40–45 minutes directly on top of the hot tray. If after 35 minutes the pastry is getting too dark, you can turn down to 180°C/fan 160°C/gas 4 and cover loosely with foil.

Leave to cool for 10 minutes before digging in.

# thanks

Nothing seems sweeter than writing a whole entire book about baking and truthfully there is a joy that I have found in writing this book that has made me realize what I love about baking and what it does for me apart from produce something sweet to eat.

I want to thank the person who decided that throwing some butter, eggs, flour and sugar together would be a good idea, because, boy, were you right, whoever you are, however far back in history you are from. Thank you! You will not read this or know of this, but we all thank you for the gift that is cake!

Thank you to our recipe tester, Katy, for the high-lighting, the note-making and the deleting of my repetitive words, but most of all thank you for the little notes on top that would read 'that was delicious' – as that is what really makes me happy!

Thank you, Chris Terry, for your beautiful photo-graphy. You are hired for your art *and* your dry sense of humour, as a package, so remember to put that on top of your packing list.

Thank you, Georgia Glynn Smith of N5 Studios.

To Rob Allison and Rosie MacKean, thank you for all the work you guys put in to getting the food prim, proper and photo-ready every single time. Thanks for not hating me when I say, 'Shall we do that one again?'.

To Roya, for your beautiful eye and attention to detail, thank you.

Anne, just always there, tapping, meddling, eating and repeating!

Thank you, Dan and Ione, for being as excited about this book as I was and for believing in it always. Dan, while you just keep powering through the food, Ione and I will be all over the spreadsheets!

Thank you to the entire team, especially Bea for our back and forth, it never annoys me, I promise, and Sarah for coming up with the most extraordinary designs, I am wowed every time! Thank you to Claire Bush, Laura Nicol, Beth O'Rafferty, Agatha Russell, Annie Lee, Gail Jones, Dan Prescott-Bennett, Heather B and everyone else for being a part of this mammoth process: we did it!

Thank you all, we have worked tirelessly to breathe joy into the book and bring it well and truly to life. For the exchanged emails in the wee hours of the night. For looking at the same thing over and over and over again till all you see is a blur. For those who have eaten, dropped and amended recipes.

Thank you, Abdal, Musa, Dawud and Maryam: for always eating cake, for as long as you will eat cake, I will bake it!

# index

**michael joseph**

UK | USA | Canada | Ireland | Australia
India | New Zealand | South Africa

Michael Joseph is part of the Penguin
Random House group of companies
whose addresses can be found at
global.penguinrandomhouse.com.

Penguin
Random House
UK

First published in Great Britain by
Michael Joseph, 2020
011

By arrangement with the BBC
BBC Logo copyright © BBC, 1996
The BBC logo is a registered trademark
of the British Broadcasting Corporation
and is used under licence

The moral right of the author has been
asserted

Set in Bauer Grotesk OT

Colour reproduction by Altaimage Ltd
Printed in Italy by Printer Trento Ltd S.r.L.

A CIP catalogue record for this book is
available from the British Library

ISBN: 978-0-241-39661-2

www.greenpenguin.co.uk